PRISONER OF GENDER
A Transsexual and the System

Katherine Johnson
and
Stephanie Castle

PERCEPTIONS PRESS
Vancouver, B.C.

Copyright © 1997 Katherine Johnson and Stephanie Castle

Canadian Cataloguing in Publication Data

Johnson, Katherine A. (Katherine Ann), 1949-
Prisoner of gender

Includes index.
ISBN 1-895590-18-3

1. Johnson, Katherine A. (Katherine Ann), 1949- 2.
Transsexuals--Canada--Biography. 3. Prisoners--Canada--
Biography. 4. Prison administration--Canada. 5. Prisoners--
Medical care--Canada. I. Castle, Stephanie. II. Title.
HQ77.8.J63A3 1995   305.3   C95-910828-9

Cover art by Catherine Hamel
Typesetting by Jean Robinson
Printed in Canada by Fleming Printing Ltd., Victoria, B.C.

Published by Perceptions Press
              8415 Granville Street
              Box 46
              Vancouver, B.C. V6P 4Z9
(Perceptions Press is an imprint of Cordillera Publishing Company)

Table of Contents

iii

Foreword

L ittle has come out of the Canadian prison system by way of
literature which conveys the prisoner's point of view. This is
particularly the case where it is expressed by the prisoner, and
voices hopes and fears and speaks objectively of feelings and
responses to prison society and a management system which at
times appears itself imprisoned by its own bureaucratic red tape
and inflexibility.

Seemingly our society has come a long way since
medieval times when prisons were associated with maximum
brutality and torture. In many instances a sentence to a term in
prison was a condemnation to a living death. In spite of this
when one reads the chilling, horrific account in this book, it is
easy enough to conclude that we have made little progress in the
handling of some aspects of prison life.

Doubly unfortunate for the transsexual prisoner,
burdened with a medical condition which is still not widely
understood, is often badly misrepresented, and is roundly
condemned by many elements in society for wholly inappropriate
reasons, a stay in prison will eliminate nothing and can be
guaranteed to aggravate the condition further.

Transsexualism is a condition which never responds to
any persuasion that it simply should go away, like a bad cold
ought to quickly leave a healthy body. Without question it is a
lifetime affliction more likely to intensify than diminish as the
person grows older.

One of the worst aspects remains. It is that a total failure
exists, within many elements of society, to comprehend that
transsexualism is a medical condition which when treated
adequately can result in a rehabilitation which brings about a
better, happier and more fulfilled person. In an imperfect world it

is a frustrating, debilitating and socially destructive condition when ignored, or is labelled as a fetishistic, bizarre fixation which the affected individual chooses.

In society's tribal traditions and beliefs, we sometimes tend to categorize sufferers from unusual conditions in such a way that the person effectively becomes less human or incapable of making their own choices and no worse example of this exists than in our prison system in its handling of transsexual cases.

The litany of brutalities, human indignities, terror, horror and dangers which this story unfolds are extreme examples of a system which aggravates rather than soothes, which distorts rather than rehabilitates. At the end of a lengthy and costly term in prison, too often the prisoner is cast back into society, crippled mentally and often physically. In such circumstances the prisoner becomes the victim and thus a further drain on the resources of society.

Katherine Johnson's honest and unvarnished portrayal of a life effectively wasted deserves attention from all who have an interest in bettering a woefully inadequate system, and understanding an equally misunderstood human condition. The reader I am sure will conclude, as I have done, that society has an expectation of better solutions to extremely vexing questions and the prison inmate, regardless of the circumstances, has a right to dignity and freedom from cruel and unusual punishment regardless of whether it be at the hand of the prison system or fellow inmates.

This book, far from resorting to sensationalism, deserves an honoured place in the field of literature dealing with transsexualism within our correctional system.

Daine B. Halley
Vancouver, B.C.
August 19, 1996

To Don

"Ours was not to be"

Acknowledgements

I wish to acknowledge the role of Patricia Diewold, friend and psychologist at the Vancouver Hospital Gender Dysphoria Clinic, who brought us two authors together. I also wish to thank Stephanie Castle for her careful, painstaking attention and at all times sympathetic and supportive attitude as the principal writer of the contents of this book.

Thanks are due also to Professor Michael Jackson of the Faculty of Law at the University of British Columbia, Blaine Beemer at Vancouver Hospital and Gayle Roberts, all of whom brought their specialist knowledge to bear on the final manuscript. There were others who in one way and another made a contribution but for reasons of their own preferred to remain unnamed.

Finally, thanks also to my sister Carolyn for her quiet patience and encouragement. All along, as my oldest friend, she has been one of the few lifetime supports on whom I could rely.

Katherine Johnson

Explanatory Note

This book represents the joint efforts of two authors each tackling the subject from a rather different viewpoint. We had some debate as to the best and most understandable way in which to present it. We concluded it would be best to get Katherine Johnson's story out in the simplest most straightforward manner, uncluttered by argument or comments which might detract from the main thrust. This is done in Part I.

Part II has been kept for Stephanie Castle's extensive comments and explanations, and the variety of documents from which quotation has been made.

By developing this separation we feel that a complex subject will be a little less complex. We also ask the reader to allow for some degree of repetition. In dealing with a subject like this one tends to come back to the same factors, but by different routes.

The degree to which Stephanie Castle's personal experiences have relevance has been the subject of differing degrees of response from pre-publication readers. The fact that this is Katherine's story is readily acknowledged. In the end after distilling all points of view we decided that certain of Stephanie's experience related personal recollections should not be eliminated as they could be said to represent an insider's highly specialised point of view. As well, they provided a basis for justification of some of Kathy's positions and backing for explanations as to how and why a person may be expected to react in given circumstances. If one has been there and endured the experience that provides a yardstick which even the most accomplished professional cannot completely claim as his or her own.

The acid test we used was to make our judgement solely on the basis of asking if the examples set out can add to the lay reader's limited knowledge and understanding of what transsexualism actually is. We also had to bear in mind that this book in many instances will be the first that readers will have read on the entire spectrum of the subjects we have covered. In the end authors have to stand behind their work. That is the judgement we have made and we will stand behind ours for better or worse.

K.J. & S.C.

Introduction

S he walked towards me. A tall, slender human being in her forties who, in spite of everything which will unfold here, is still a surprisingly spritely looking woman. The problems and challenges of her past and those she still has to face would have crippled or even killed a lesser person. In the shaded light of her apartment her face showed a quiet and serene beauty which gave a hint of how things might have been far different in her life, if nature had not made its mistake and had instead seen her born female. Her good looks contradicted the hard and brutal life from which she had so recently been released.

This is Kathy Johnson, born male. Her mother died at the early age of 30 when Kathy was just three and a half years old. Her indifferent father, good provider though he was in wage-earning terms, married again, and it seems that with the entry of a new stepmother into her life, Kathy's troubles really began. By the time she was 11 she was already rated as an incorrigible young hellion and from then on in a series of escalations she graduated to burglary, addictive drugs and bank robbery. As a result she spent 30 of her 46 years accumulating a prison record and acquiring the reputation of a hardened criminal.

Kathy's basic problem is that she was born with the condition of gender dysphoria, a sometimes disabling illness more commonly known as transsexualism and to the unaffected, one of the strangest and most misunderstood of all human conditions. To some it is akin to witchcraft, being treated with a similar degree of intolerance and the urge to punish for punishment's sake. To others it is as stigmatizing as the leprosy of old.

I repeat: she was "born" with it. Its complex origins start at a point in the individual's foetal existence. Exactly where and why is still a matter of educated theory, but that it is biological is hardly now in doubt, and it may even have genetic origins.

Once established as a part of the human system it never leaves as it is in every sense a lifetime condition. Usually the condition first becomes apparent in early childhood, but just what it is, is usually quite mystifying in the mind of a young child. From then on it influences their lives in a variety of subtle and not-so-subtle ways, and in turn makes the individual more responsive to the negative aggravations caused by outside societal, family and general environmental factors. In extreme form and provided the right combination of circumstances exist, it can be the basis for a very stormy life.

What follows is essentially a history of fundamental gender dysphoric influences within Kathy and the disastrous consequences of her treatment and responses. It is also a condemnation of the Canadian federal prison system, or to use its present day pseudonymic title, Corrections Service Canada.

A transsexual's sensitivities, whether biologically male or female, are extraordinarily deep, and probably a good deal more so than will be found in the average unaffected person. They can create a living hell for the sufferer and sometimes the people around him or her. How he or she handles or is affected by all these diverse factors influences his or her quality of life, and for some, including Kathy, the price has been very high.

Yes, very high indeed. Kathy is still legally a man, and even owning up to that fact is painful for her. She still has a penis, which has always been an abhorrence to her. She would much prefer to substitute a vagina. She does not look like a man, she does not sound like a man, she does not present as a man and philosophically she is not a man. She is very natural in a feminine way and does not put on any contrived or mincing effeminacies.

Her face shows no significant masculine features and her natural breasts protrude discretely under her sweater. Hidden by her clothes are the telltale scars of suicide attempts on both her neck and her arms as well as the needle marks of the period in her life when she sought solace in heroin. Hidden also are the results of a successful castration which she herself undertook with surgical skill and a singularity of purpose which one can understand, even if horrified, when the circumstances are fully explained.

Once in the prison system her life went from one level in hell to another, each more total than the last. She suffered gang rape and every conceivable abuse. Solitary confinement to get away from the turmoil her presence created was often welome. A suicide attempt brought her so close to death that she believes she actually died for a short while and even now she suffers permanent mental injury as a result.

Sometimes brutal prison guards, through every level of the management system right up to the responsible federal minister, combined to frustrate her efforts to let the world know of her crying need for understanding and some supportive treatment for her gender dysphoric condition. She confronted all this almost alone and with only the aid of a few sympathetic fellow prisoners and outsiders.

Kathy does not deny her culpability and is not without a great deal of regret for a life largely wasted. She has accepted her record and society's requirements that she repay her debt, which she has done. She committed crimes, she paid the price and she makes no excuses. She makes no representations which would make the imprisonment of the wrongdoer lighter, the issue she takes up deals entirely with health, misplacement within the system and the total incapacity of the prison management structure to accommodate itself to anything other than a rigid, implacable and doctrinaire set of rules which her case has proven to be out of date and plainly wrong.

What we offer are explanations of characteristic behaviour patterns and the complex manner in which these ill-fitted the shortcomings of a penal system which was never designed with the idea of adequately accommodating transsexuals. Her stoicism in the face of perpetual ongoing adversity indicates that there is a very strong character underneath that is determined to rise above all this and still achieve her life-long aim of achieving womanhood as closely as this can be accomplished.

Even though there are notable exceptions among the professional caregiving community, it is often said that no one understands a transsexual like another transsexual, and this is largely true. My own passage through life has been in all regards a total contrast to that of Kathy. There is, however, one identical circumstance—I am also a former transsexual. I use the word "former" to indicate that due to a proper course of psychiatric counselling, hormone therapy and surgery, I am now legally, functionally and philosophically a woman. The philosophic basis of this has always been present as that is a feature of the incongruency between body and mind which distinguishes the condition of transsexualism. The word "biologically" is missing from the above and that is because the fundamental biology or chromosomal blueprint which accompanied my conception cannot be altered. However, I have now achieved the inner peace of mind that is the ultimate aim of all gender dysphoria sufferers. Even though the circumstances of our two lives have been so radically different, I can feel for Kathy and have an insight into the hellish inferno which has been such a big part of her life.

It is the hope of both of us that this book will help open up some new avenues of understanding in the official and the public mind. We hope that the perception will grow that we never seek our transsexual condition as it finds us before birth. Whatever the selection process within nature which brings about transsexualism, it appears to arise like some minute event which is still unmeasurable. We who are affected risk obliteration by the onrush of a largely unsympathetic or indifferent society because of our condition of transsexualism, as we search for answers to the question "why me?" We do take some comfort from the evidence that human rights thinking is gradually moving in our favour. But little will change unless we ourselves do something positive to let our plight be known and insist on change. Kathy's sacrifices did eventually get the message across that her plight was real and before the end of this book evidence will be presented that conditions for transsexuals trapped within the system have changed only slightly for the better. Neither this nor a fully documented recital of the responses of near-blind officialdom relieves that same system of a terrible moral and probable potential legal liability for gross negligence, mismanagement and needless abuse amounting to a form of torture, throughout the period of her tenure in prison, as it relates to a medical condition ignored and denied.

What it all adds up to is cruel and unusual punishment in terms of her citizen's rights under the Canadian Charter of Rights and Freedoms, but there are also broader issues involved. These include a need for a legal definition of transsexualism based on, but expanded from, the simple medical definition set out and discussed in Chapter Eight. A legal definition would need to set out the rights of the individual in his or her special circumstances and also create a proper societal basis for dealing with such people, including those whose fate it is to spend time in prison.

That it is a plight cannot be overstated. Those who fall between the cracks for whatever reason are often treated cruelly by the system in its broader meaning. The system is government, our institutions, our churches, our schools and media, our legal and medical professions, and ourselves, the ordinary man and woman in the street. We are riven by our doubts and uncertainties, ignorant and prejudiced often for reasons we cannot adequately define for even in our modern society, a sort of tribalism still runs strongly just like it did thousands of years ago when mankind was supposedly emerging from its primitive existence.

We know this book and its strident message will stir controversy, but however the matters touched upon may encourage sympathy or indignation it will remain an indictment which demands explanation, review and a whole new attitude, particularly in the organs of government, to the perplexing challenge presented by transsexualism, a modern day affliction which has probably been around since the beginnings of civilization. It is a socially destructive condition, but it is not the transsexual who makes it that way. It is our reactive society with its demands that minorities conform even if nature decrees otherwise.

We also know there will be those who do not want their consciences disturbed and those who have no conscience. There will be those in a perpetual state of denial. There will be those too ready to condemn, as they deny their own shortcomings and there will be those who will swear by some God-given perception of their own that we as transsexuals are bound for perpetual purgatory. We say, that is Kathy and myself, that this is nonsense and if society cannot wake up to the fact that transsexualism is a genuine definable and treatable condition, then it is society itself, including the so-called pillars of the establishment, which stands condemned by any standard of ethics or common humanity.

Stephanie Castle

PART ONE

by

Katherine Johnson

Prisoner of Gender

Chapter One

The Early Years:
An Apprenticeship for Crime

Before losing consciousness I caught a glimpse of my life blood pumping out through my jugular vein in great eight-foot impulses. Fascination is the wrong word; perhaps horror more correctly describes the consequences of my single act of cutting my own jugular as I momentarily realized that I was on my way to a certain death just as I had planned. I curled up on my bunk as life oozed out of me, and thought to myself, "Finally I will have peace."

As I slipped into a nether world between life and death I had the sensation in some way of either seeing or feeling the escape of my spirit from my now apparently dead body where it hovered overhead. I could see it in an unreal way with whatever consciousness I had left. In spite of my overall condition my brain still functioned. I recall being found and placed on a stretcher by a medical crew who whisked me to hospital. My brain could still register the snippets of conversation which filtered through.

"This one's dead" was the comment of the ambulance man as I was wheeled into emergency. The attending doctor took no notice of the ambulance man's comment as he called for two flasks of blood, after shining a light in my eyes. I gather from this that he could tell that my brain was still functioning. Slowly consciousness returned and from this point on I was to spend three months recovering in hospital. Things would never be the same for me again as oxygen deprivation and ultra-low blood pressure did permanent damage to my brain.

This was not to be my only brush with death. Before and after this attempt, I was close to and witnessed jail beatings and shootings, one of which was the plainest murder imaginable. I made other suicide attempts, at least two of which brought me as close to death as the cutting of my jugular.

For some strange reason suicide attempts which should have been successful failed. I sometimes feel that the Good Lord somehow wanted to preserve me, perhaps to eventually tell my story. Death would have been a welcome release from the hell in which I somehow existed, and after each attempt I resented the efforts which were made to save me.

When I refer to hell I am not directly referring to the prison system, brutal though it could be and frequently was. I am thinking in terms of the perverse side of my nature, and the contradictions and ambivalence which existed in my mind like a can of seething worms. It took me a long time to understand the nature of gender dysphoria in the form it took within me. My earliest recollections include a vague memory of my mother's face before she died and my natural inclination was to lean towards my older sister, my playmate and first friend, whose instinct was to protect and look after me. In this early period of my life when I was deprived of my own mother, my father was in need of someone to look after the "kids," so advertised for a housekeeper who in due course became my stepmother. My father, although an honest man, was like so many fathers, distant and aloof from his children. He did his job as a carpenter and brought home the earnings which supported his family and home. As a good provider he felt his duty ended there, and that it was the role of a woman to bring up his children. Maybe this was so, and was certainly widely accepted in society as being a feminine duty beyond anything that should be expected from a father. In adopting this attitude I believe he set the seal on what was to become the first of many crosses I had to bear. To blame someone else for all my problems is not my purpose, but this was in fact the trigger which started the whole parade of adverse circumstances in my life.

My new stepmother was a stern disciplinarian, and like so many of her type, discipline either overstated the need or was unfairly applied. But discipline with brutality and a sadistic twist was another thing. Her ideas of punishment terrorised me: typically one such was to have me kneel on hard grains of rice spread on the polished kitchen floor until she decreed that I had learned a valuable lesson over some infraction such as not knowing how to properly tie my boot laces at the age of four.

A clue as to the true nature of my underlying personality was perhaps to be found in the fact that I loved playing girls' games with my sister and her neighbourhood girlfriends. These included skipping and playing such games as hopscotch. These games would go on in our backyard often while my father was working at his favourite hobby of tinkering with his car. I was too young to appreciate what was feminine and masculine. The need for such a division never crossed my mind. I merely moved in the direction which seemed natural to me without any realization that I was crossing one of those societal stereotypes so precious today.

"Dougie, why don't you go and play with the boys instead of playing girls' games," my father said on more than one occasion as he literally dragged me over to some neighbourhood boys who probably held me in contempt as a result. He could not know that even then this sort of mild admonishment built resentment in my overly sensitive mind. Like so many boys, I believe in looking back, my natural desire was to have that special relationship with my father which reflected my masculine instinct to grow up in his masculine image. But without warmth, and lacking encouragement and adequate channels of communication, any such desire contradicted the established feminine aspects of my personality, which even then were showing through in my tendency to seek the warmth of the friendship and companionship of my sister and her friends. In spite of this need, there were many times when I just wanted to be alone with my private thoughts. This is a feature I am told of many transsexually affected people.

In most ways I cannot blame my father. It merely reflected the common belief, then as now, that boys should not be brought up as sissies, and the way to avoid this was to knock the soft spots off. Lots of work tasks, a healthy interest in sports, the ability to stand up and protect oneself, maybe a spell in the army or at sea, were all masculine disciplines regarded as worthwhile and to be encouraged, and for normal boys the system, under a good father and supportive mother, could develop strong and admirable character traits.

But what happens when a boy with equally strong basic, but for the most part hidden, feminine traits shows up. A distortion in the personality is a consequence as the boy seeks to accommodate himself to masculine expectations which contradict his mental core identity as a female person. This is a good example of gender dysphoria, and all the brutal punishment in the world will not drive it out of the subject. In fact, brutality or abuse in whatever form has only one result: it drives the dysphoria in ever deeper as the subject finds that his only escape from the realities of his life is to the oasis in his fantasy mind. A horse can be flogged until he is dead, but nothing will drive him to drink water against his will. A transsexual child finds himself in much the same position except that he cannot diagnose his own condition any more than the parent can understand what it is that besets the child with often such devilish consequences.

Behaviour patterns of a very complex nature seem to be a natural consequence. The child seeks to fit into the expectations of society, not knowing what is the fire that burns in his brain and tells him that he is something a good deal different from the visual truth of his sexuality. He senses he is female but soon finds that females like him with penises are not regarded as being acceptable as girls within society. He later rationalizes this and probably concludes that perhaps he is a female in a male body, or if this is not an acceptable idea, then at least the God who is supposed to have made us all made a dreadful error and that the real intention of nature was that he should have been born in the other sex.

One aspect of all this is that an understanding of society's rejection of the notion that one could even think of being of the opposite sex becomes paramount. The lesson is driven home again and again by early admonitions "to play with the boys" which as I mentioned came from my father. This is reinforced over time by the jeers of boys at school, should one show any temptation towards the female point of view or sympathy with that attractive race, all the girls of one's own age group. Following this comes the alien world of the adult so often hostile to anyone different from themselves and fed by official ignorance and prejudice and the attitude of the media which has seldom shown much knowledge of the true nature of gender dysphoria.

What is the consequence of all these social pressures? Self-inflicted repression, a bottling up of emotions, an apparent deadening of the personality, and an inability to give vent to one's true feelings. When these are taken into account alongside typical gender dysphoric sensitivities, a tug o' war takes place in the mind of the sufferer, so that usually his only escape is to resort to whatever peace is to be found in his own internal fantasy world or perhaps some degree of crossdressing.

Self-repression is one of the two worst and most painful symptoms of gender dysphoria and is probably the single most important factor in driving the sufferer from the condition to doing crazy irrational acts, many of which in my own case had such disastrous effects throughout my life.

The other symptom is chronic anxiety so severe at times that it leaves the sufferer stressed out and exhausted. Anxiety mounts on anxiety and frustration, breeding an attitude of depression and complete helplessness. Is it any wonder that for some the only answer is suicide? Believe me, the prospect of deliverance by death from all this can look unusually attractive when all else has failed.

* * * * *

I was born April 16, 1948, in Vancouver as Douglas Melvin Johnson. I followed my sister Carolyn by two years. Our mother, Alice Garnet Johnson, died November 3, 1951, in Vancouver General Hospital at the age of 30 of cancer which she probably was already developing when she was carrying me. Our father, John Melvin Johnson, has also been dead for some years now, but my stepmother who shall remain unnamed is still living. She is not a part of my life anymore except for a host of bad memories and none that are good. My parents were, I believe, of Norwegian descent, which should come as no great surprise as there are large Scandinavian ethnic communities on the West Coast.

Following my mother's death we two children were sent to live with our grandmother. That might have turned out to be a good move, but regrettably Grannie died suddenly five days after we arrived. From there we went to an aunt who was a tyrant, but that was not to last long as we were then passed to my father's brother. To say that all this shifting around was profoundly disturbing to the two of us would be an understatement, but when we went back to our own home it was to be confronted by a housekeeper who quickly became our new stepmother, and thus the circle of early disaster was completed.

I went to a primary school on the east side of Vancouver. Tall and thin for my age, I was uncomfortable with the other boys. As if like a lame dog, they sensed this and took it out on me particularly when it became apparent that I could not adjust to physical education and taking showers with the other boys. I was overcome by embarrassment and shame of my naked body. The result was that I played "hookey" most of the time and only managed to reach grade three after being held back for extra years, before being finally declared incorrigible and beyond help.

Knowing what I know today I have to wonder how any parents could acquiesce in such a judgement, but on the other hand I have to take into account the attitude of this dominant new stepmother and the subsequent weakness of my father who effectively abdicated his role as head of the family.

I first got into trouble with the law at the age of nine and it was at about this time that I undertook my first experimentation with crossdressing, "borrowing" some of my sister's underclothes. Being as deeply disturbed as I was, I discovered that wearing her underwear had a strangely soothing effect on me.

At the age of ten I was placed in a foster home. I felt I was being treated unjustly and at this point I want to state that so many of these foster homes are run as businesses by the foster parents. In my view they are treated as dumping grounds by the authorities who are only interested in the external gloss and finding a place to park their charges. The one I went to housed a group of problem children. There was a lot of physical abuse and no warmth in the relationship so that the children tended to huddle together as a means of self-protection. They were all candidates for the street life sooner or later and in fact some like me had already been on the street. In these circumstances there is a bonding between the kids who come to regard each other as their family to the exclusion of others not in their peer group.

Very shortly after I was placed in the foster home, I ran away for the first time and made straight for my father's home. He was determined to return me to the foster home so I ran into the bathroom, locked myself in, and slashed both wrists three times. My father broke the door open and took me to emergency to be stitched up and returned to the foster home. I ran away again and this time managed to live by my wits on my own for a time. I think back to that period and wonder how many parents would have taken a similar view. As a runaway child I locked myself in the bathroom, cutting both wrists quite severely, and yet my father and stepmother did not see it as any major issue. Very odd!! But I am sure that responsible parents would have asked some intelligent questions as to why an obviously deeply troubled ten-year old boy acted in the manner he did. Once again there was cause for some calm and informed reasoning by a professional consultant, but any such idea evidently escaped them.

Petty theft became a pattern as by now I was largely living on and off the street. Favourite targets for food were local supermarkets from which I stole stuff like chocolate bars. I would climb onto the roof of a typical one-story building using the fire escape, find a trap door and break into the warehouse section. I would grab a selection of my favourite brands and anything else in the way of candy which was within easy reach. It was not exactly a balanced diet, but rich in sugar and other things like palm or coconut oil—all of which I needed far less than a proper diet.

When I was caught I was sent to a juvenile detention home. After a spell of the style of discipline that was handed out, I came out again for a brief interlude to again be caught for stealing, so this time at the age of 11, I was shipped off to Brannan Lake Correctional School near Nanaimo, B.C.

I was to have three spells in Brannan Lake and in each instance I escaped. It was here that I underwent my first brush with sexual and physical abuse at the hands of older inmates. Brutality on the part of supervisory staff was commonplace and on one occasion I was hit across the face by the school's psychologist as he accused me of every bad thing imaginable regardless of the truth. He was interviewing me and I was trying to explain in my limited way what it was which I felt motivated me so negatively. The treatment made me feel helplessly angry, deeply resentful and inadequate.

The psychologist suggested that I be put into the boxing ring to "make a man out of me." I would cover my face and be used as a human punching bag. Then I would run from the ring only to be pushed back in. There were several of these boxing ring episodes until I finally became aware that the only escape was to do something which would place me in the hole, segregated as much as possible, living somewhat like a rat always on the lookout for danger.

On my third stay at Brannan Lake, each stay being about one year, I made my final escape from the hole at age 14. I had been out cleaning and the guard forgot about me. I soon heard him snoring and I peeked around the corner, seeing the big ring of keys lying on the desk in front of him. I knew these keys would enable me to be free as I sneaked over to the desk and very quietly lifted them. I slowly turned the key in the door and silently made for the next door which led to the front offices and the main door, freedom and back to Vancouver.

The initial interview with the psychologist was the first time that I tried to reveal to another human being a hint as to what was gnawing at my vitals. Had he exercised any intelligence or understanding he would have listened instead of abusing me. This was 1961 and by now transsexual operations had received plenty of publicity over the previous ten years or so. It had filtered through to me that I myself was perhaps transsexual which might have accounted for my greater comfort with girls, my withdrawn attitude and discomfort with boys and my fear of men as, after all, I had run into very few of the latter who had shown any kindness or mercy.

While at Brannan Lake I had managed to complete grades three through to six. After Brannan Lake I was transferred to Oakalla Prison at age 14, (illegally, I might add, for two months until I had reached 15 years), and was then moved up to adult court and sentenced to two years definite and two years indefinite for escapes and housebreaking and entering. Let me say that to this point my housebreaking escapades were primarily to provide myself with food. I was not into taking valuables, being mainly interested in the contents of the fridge. I would help myself to bread and make a sandwich with whatever I could find that took my fancy. I would coolly sit down at the kitchen table, enjoy my food, and leave the debris, maybe a used glass with milk stains, or crumbs as telltales of my visit.

For my sentence of two years definite and two years indefinite I was sent to Haney Correctional Institute, where I served three years. Normally with good behaviour I would have been out after two years, but such instances when I had to rebel at staff in order to get into solitary caused them to determine that I was a bad lot and so I remained an extra year. While I was there I did manage to complete grades seven and eight. All these institutions had communal showers which made me feel very uncomfortable. I would try to time a shower to when no one else was present, but just the same the entire ablution area was open to all eyes. The sinks and toilets were right there and in the latter case only had two 24-inch deep swinging doors in front of them. There was never any privacy and this was emotionally very draining for me. I know the reason for this has to do with full supervision of prisoners at all times, quite likely a necessity, but still something which heightened my ever present embarrassment.

It was in Haney when I first noticed my pubic hair. Also, a slight fuzz was appearing on my face and this became very depressing because I knew that eventually I would have to shave. In my heart and mind I was a girl not a boy, and the thought of whiskers and body hair made me shudder. When I went to bed I usually cried myself to sleep. While there at Haney a very major amount of sexual abuse towards me occurred on an almost daily basis, except when I managed to get into segregation where I would at least have some peace in my own company.

When I was not in jail I frequently spent the nights sleeping in the crawlspace under my father's house. I could not enter the home proper because of fear of my stepmother who was in complete control of my father and everything else which concerned family matters. In the circumstances I was a most unwelcome and disturbing visitor so would quietly sneak under the house after dark, gaining entry through a small side door. I slept on a bed of old newspapers and sneaked away in the same manner in the morning. I gather that this make-shift bed was only found some years later.

It was also in my fourteenth year which would be 1962 that I made my first acquaintance with heroin. Like any other regular user I soon became addicted, which increased my need to steal in order to support my habit. In the street scene as an addict I found myself completely accepted by the other addicts which was probably the first time in my life that I had gained acceptance by any group of people. Heroin gave me temporary comfort and a degree of security with some freedom from the constant turmoil in my mind.

Four months after I was released from Haney Correctional I was back on the street again and quickly returned to heroin. I was then sentenced to eighteen months in Oakalla at the age of 18. The guys there were much older and inevitably more sexual and physical abuse occurred. In an effort to offset my constant depression and overcome my shyness and obvious sensitivity I started to use make-up, which I got from the girls in the "cathouse," as the women's jail was called. The reader will understandably question my wisdom in this matter, but all through prison wearing make-up did boost my morale and I felt happier, but the men took it as a come-on, that I was on the hunt for sex, that I was wearing my make-up for them, when nothing could have been further from the truth. However, it is also an indication of the sometimes overpowering driving influence within a transsexual and the need for expression or an outlet. It is the lack of consideration for the consequences which will likely make an unaffected reader regard this as being wholly irrational.

I suffered a great deal of anxiety and when I couldn't get medication to calm me I would slash my arms. These were not suicide attempts but rather calming events. After I had lost two or three pints of blood I would feel very calm and mellow. I would then get help to go to the hospital to be stitched up and remain there, continuing to feel calm for several days. It was also a relief from being housed with men.

At the age of 19, my father and stepmother came to visit me, and seeing me clothed in a custom-tailored satin outfit and full make-up, became quite concerned. They later phoned Dr. Guy Richmond of Oakalla who called me to his office for an interview which in turn led to a referral to a much-respected doctor at the University of British Columbia medical school. For the very first time I was able to talk to someone with an understanding of transsexualism and his diagnosis was that it was probably just a phase I was going through and encouraged me to become involved in sports. That was like suggesting to a person with my disposition that I try diving into a barrel of burning oil and, equally as bad, whatever judgement was formed by this expert was the result of one interview alone. Now, no matter how brilliant this doctor might have been or still is, to slough me off on the basis of one interview, when it must have been obvious to even the most junior doctor that my symptoms were more complex than a common cold, was in my view a dereliction of his duty as a professional. Maybe he viewed me as a useless criminal hardly worth his time and consideration, but for all the good he did his opinion was worthless.

Had there been any understanding at that time, there might have been some worthwhile conclusions reached tending to confirm that my rebelliousness and antisocial attitudes were in some way related to the deep dissatisfaction which I could not adequately describe, let alone properly understand, which were a part of my condition of transsexualism. Buoyed on the one hand that someone had at last perhaps seen something in me which I had long felt, it was a terrible letdown to once again have the hope that something might be done to ease my anxiety and misery. Instead my hopes were dashed to the ground.

Unfortunately this was to be the pattern over much of my remaining life in prison. Reports from established specialists in their fields of psychiatry and psychology were obtained at the expense of the taxpayer and after being made, confirming my own personal understanding of my problem, they simply went into a docket to be ignored, or worse still effectively countermanded by prison doctors who refused to act on specialist recommendations.

Shortly after this interview with the specialist I was feeling greatly disturbed. A day or two later as we were walking out to the fields to work I broke away from the other 20-30 prisoners. I ran up the hill to a perimeter fence where a guard was on duty with a shotgun! I started climbing the fence and screamed to the guard, "Shoot me, shoot me!" as I climbed. I didn't want to escape, I wanted to be shot and killed.

Just as I reached the top of the fence, the warden approached in his chauffered car. He got out of his car and called to the guard, "Shoot that man." The guard looked at the warden and then looked back to me and threw his shotgun to the ground. He quit his job at Oakalla that very day. I was placed in the hole, which was under the cowbarns. At night it was hard to sleep because the cows were chained in the barn. The chains rattled and the cows stamped their feet. During the day I couldn't sleep either. The guards patrolled and if they caught you sleeping they would turn on the water hose and soak you down. We were fed eight slices of bread and a cup of water in the morning and the same at night.

The cost to the system was to mount up as they dealt in their indifferent, unfeeling, ham-handed way with my personal and desperate search for answers to my predicament, while the cost to my health was to leave me permanently impaired. If only someone in authority had had the knowledge and guts, instead of ducking responsibilities, to confront the problem as it really was instead of dealing with me as though I were a constant malingerer. The reality was that my efforts to gain some recognition of my condition were about as effective as trying to break down a concrete wall with a bouncing tennis ball.

* * * * *

16

Chapter Two

Welcome to the B.C. Pen

In 1968, at the age of 20 I entered that dreaded grey fortress at New Westminster, the British Columbia Penitentiary, then the main federal prison west of the Rockies. This time I had graduated to bank robbery as a means to support my heroin addiction. I never pulled a gun on anyone or committed any violent act. As with my housebreaking for food it was sort of low-key. I had to fill a need and I did it in the most peaceful fashion possible by simply passing a note across to the teller demanding money. Usually it worked as there was always the implied threat of a concealed weapon, perhaps a banana in a paper bag.

Hangings took place fairly frequently from the time of the Pen's opening as a prison early in the century until the death penalty was finally abolished. Today a housing estate occupies the site, but I wonder if any ghosts still hang around the neighbourhood. There were not only hangings, but killings by and of prisoners and guards.

Killing of one prisoner by another has always been a risk, as they have their own code. Stool pigeons are a natural mark, but also those who commit certain crimes, such as offences against children, are marked men from the day they enter prison, and for their own good have to be segregated. "Trannies," as they are usually referred to, are another group who are regarded as natural prey for the prison predators, and because of my insistence on my recognition as the woman I knew myself to be, I was a target from the beginning, enduring gang rape on a number of occasions. One occurred when I was trapped by four other prisoners while putting something away in a closet. Two of them held me while one performed anal rape and the other forced me to perform oral sex. Not a pretty sight for anyone, and of course by the time guards arrived to break it up, it was all over except that I was devastated. Needless to say events like this only caused the guards to shrug their shoulders, the attitude being that if you did things, or as in my case wore things, which created a provocation, then this was your problem.

Death threats by guards were a given if anything leaked out to the public about abuse. One guard did, however, pay a high price for his abuse. He lost both hands in an explosive booby trap which had been set for him by a prisoner whose specialty had been safecracking. One friend of mine, Wally Brass, was killed by guards in a segregation unit in 1969, but just what the circumstances were I never found out, as it was all hushed up.

Moving ahead of sequence a little, one of the most notorious events in the history of B.C. Pen occurred in 1974. A small group of rebellious prisoners, led by Andy Bruce, took prison classification officer Mary Steinhouser as a hostage in a prison escape attempt. This case made the national headlines, unlike many prison events which were hushed up. Ms. Steinhouser, as is so often the case, was a convenient but innocent victim of an event which likely came to her like a bolt out of the blue.

Bruce was ready to surrender as he crouched behind Mary. She had her hands up screaming, "Don't shoot, they want to surrender." That was not good enough for one guard. He fired directly at the poor woman, shooting her through the heart. As she collapsed he then fired at Bruce, hitting him with several shots which caused severe injury, although not fatal.

When this hostage-taking took place, as in all major disturbances, prisoners are locked in their cells. I was in the hospital unit when the hostage-taking occurred, due to a very serious attempt to kill myself. I had sliced my left arm from wrist to elbow and to about half its depth, rather like a loaf of bread sliced lengthwise and opened up. This was followed by one-inch cuts from side to side, so I was very sure that I would die and the torture would be over, but that was not to be! Three hundred stitches later I awoke in the prison hospital. The doctor decided to put me on 30 mg injections of Demerol every four hours and this went on for 33 days. (For those who do not know Demerol, an opiate, is in the same group of drugs as morphine and heroin.)

The doctor, however, was in a state of shock because of the severe damage I did, and he just wanted to keep me drugged in the hospital where I could be watched. After 33 days of Demerol I was addicted so they took care of the withdrawal symptoms by giving me Talwin compound, a synthetic morphine, which they then reduced on a daily basis.

A week after the hostage-taking Andy Bruce, who was a friend, came into the prison hospital following discharge from Royal Columbian Hospital at New Westminster, where his wounds had been dealt with. Guards, doctors and nurses are as might be expected, very unsympathetic to hostage-takers so that Bruce received very little for his pain. I managed to sneak him some Talwin occasionally.

Following the hostage-taking, and the shooting of Mary Steinhouser, there were several enquiries by outside authorities. The responsible guard mixed his gun in a box with many others, trying to cover up the fact that it was he who did the deed, and naturally the other guards present would not say who fired the fatal shot into Mary Steinhouser and followed it with wounding

Andy Bruce. However, after these enquiries were completed the responsible guard was known, but there was no punishment. They just transferred him to Ottawa, gave him a gun for his own protection and a job to teach other guards marksmanship!

When I left the hospital I went back up to the "penthouse." The penthouse consists of four ranges: segregation, hole, psychiatric, and one for child molesters, rapists and rats. The guards were acting very bitterly towards prisoners after the hostage-taking and you could just feel the tension in the air.

I was in the psychiatric range and the person next door was Bruce Bird, whom I had known for some 15 years. There was a guard on the catwalk behind a screen with a .303 rifle, which was always standard practice. When the doors opened for a brief period to get meals, I asked Bruce for some tobacco. We stood there with him putting some in a bag. Suddenly I heard a shell being put into the .303, followed by the locking of the bolt in place, and then the guard screamed "in the cells right now" and at almost the same instant a loud bang.

The bullet struck the cement and steel between our heads, shattering into fragments, some of which along with pieces of broken concrete embedded themselves in our scalps and faces. The dust which got into the eyes was the most painful and needless to say it was several hours before we got medical attention.

There are some very sadistic guards in the prison system. At that point in time all that was required to get a job as a guard was to have a Grade 12 education. A number had rackets, one being drug-dealing. This sort of prison racketeering has not changed. According to a recent television news report aired on BCTV (April 1995) one of the prison officials himself attested to the fact that drugs move freely in Mountain prison and that some of the guards are in on the racket. Such guards become compromised in becoming a part of the underground supply system. They may become subject to blackmail and threats to take action against their family members through contacts in the underworld. Once some have partaken of the devil's nectar there is a price to pay in terms of security.

The peaceful law-abiding public know little of the drama which is a common, almost daily event in our prison system. We all know, and accept it as part of our society, that the price of crime is imprisonment and it has been this way for hundreds of years. The justification for a riot may well be mounting dissatisfaction over prison conditions, including the treatment meted out by guards. I am not suggesting that being a prison guard is an easy or attractive job and because there is one guard to a given ratio of prisoners, I suppose it is probable that there is a feeling of being outnumbered when serious trouble breaks out. There is no doubt that some prisoners become particularly savage and vengeful and I suspect that something of an "it's them or me" syndrome may develop.

One problem of course is that in the end everyone suffers for it in some way or another including innocent peaceful prisoners who are likely in the majority in the first instance. There is always a trouble-seeking element in any group and all that the peaceful types want to do is get on with their sentences and earn remission for good behaviour.

Torture was sometimes resorted to by the guards. While in Oakalla I was chained by the wrists and hung from the ceiling for several hours with my feet off the ground. When I was eventually cut down I fell in a crumpled heap and it was several days before my limbs and muscles returned to normal.

One guard used to throw razor blades into my cell. I had a history of wrist slashing, and this was deliberate provocation. Fortunately I never used any of the unwelcome blades, but this was a sample of the needling, sadistic attitude of some guards. I cannot say that all guards were bad. Many I am sure just wanted to do their shifts efficiently according to the rules and get back to their homes and families, like other normal working men, but when jobs exist which give an opportunity for taking power over others, there are always those who will be attracted. Jailbirds, as our type are often referred to, are deemed to be the dregs of society and are therefore fair game for abuse. The most abusive are those who have a natural leaning to being bullies and worse still sadists. Hitler never had any trouble in finding lots of candidates for this type of work and I know many of the same type are available to our jail systems.

From the point of view of the average prisoner, once that steel gate clangs behind you, you are caught like a rat in a trap. The purpose of imprisonment is to pay for your crimes against society and learn something about good societal behaviour in the process, which for some is more a pious hope and less of a fact than for others. I know all this as well as anyone and I do not seek to make excuses. What I do want to convey is some impression of the sense of helplessness in being at the mercy of the system. There is precious little hope of redress, protest falls mostly on deaf ears, and protests of a more forceful kind can lead to injury and death as I described earlier. The need for medical attention must become a necessity for everyone at some point. Your friendly doctor on the outside is often an unknown in prison. More likely he will be as dehumanized as the whole system is dehumanizing and maybe he even took the job because he could not succeed in the free society outside.

Aside from injuries self-inflicted from suicide attempts and injuries occurring from beatings and gang rapes, my general health was good. The one thing which maintained a constant presence was my ever-present transsexualism. Okay, shrug it off as a fixation or some lunatic idea with no real relevance. I was told I would grow out of it which in itself was an example of gross ignorance as anyone who suffers from the condition knows so well. One never grows out of it. In fact, it usually becomes more deeply entrenched as one becomes older. No one wants to deal with it in a meaningful way, least of all in the prison system where cattle were better off, as at Oakalla, than I was in the circumstances of being a transsexual prisoner. At least a milk cow would get attention from the farmer or a veterinarian when needed, but then the animal was an economic factor more valuable alive than dead from natural causes.

Transsexualism was simply not understood in the prison system and from what I can determine no one wanted to learn anything about it. It was little different with the politicians and the religious leaders. The politicians treated it as a non-event—after all it was not likely to garner many votes and could always be written off on the basis that there were far bigger challenges requiring their attention.

The main churches simply swept it under the carpet while the fundamentalists condemned it according to some biblical interpretation of their own. They had nothing to go by in the Bible as it is not even mentioned. I know that too well as the Bible was all I had to read when in solitary and I read it several times! The fundamentalists claim that the Bible is their contract with God. Just try to debate the issue with them and the barricades go up as though even the mention of transsexualism is defiling them in some way. There is no such thing as a welcome disease or medical condition, but if the condition of transsexualism is counted in then it must take a high prize for "unpopularity" in any poll taken among those who are responsible for our governance, our imprisonment or our religious well-being.

It never occurred to anyone by a process of simple logic that the root of my problem, my protest which was written off as the mad rantings of a deadbeat, a no good criminal not worthy of even the time of day, and my desire to achieve some simple peace and tranquility in my life, might just have had something to do with my gender dysphoric condition and probably had done over most of my life. In my own mind I was a woman and wanted more than anything to take the steps which would have made living life as such, a possibility.

I was not gay. In fact, I had been married for one brief period of ten months, but for self-protection in a vicious system I was forced to enter into a relationship and find a protector, a "strong man" who would look after me against the forced attentions of the prison rapists. It was either that or solitary confinement for my own good and in 30 years of imprisonment I spent 13 years confined alone in just this sort of situation. Without a combination of a protector or solitary it is doubtful if I would have even been alive today, quite apart from suicide attempts.

Give thought to earlier comments about the cost to the system of maintaining a single prisoner and then take a look at some of the other costs incurred, most of which would have been avoidable in a more enlightened regime. My suicide attempt alone when I cut my jugular and spent three months in hospital must have cost several tens of thousands in emergency, specialist and hospital care. Had I gone for gender reassignment surgery then, the cost would likely have been a lot less than the approximate $8,000 it costs today for surgery in Montreal, and what would have been the result? Legal sex change and the ability to live in the form and manner that I am convinced was meant to be but for the accident of nature when my mother was pregnant with me.

Another result would have been that they would then have had a happier more docile prisoner who could spend the rest of her sentence in a woman's institution. I would have achieved mental peace and removed myself from the tension and continuous harassment and never-ending danger in which I lived as a legal male. Equally, I believe I would have earned remission credits which I had constantly lost through seeking solitary as a means of gaining some peace.

Those who are unaffected will say that this is just so much nonsense, a figment of an overactive imagination, stand up to it like a man and take your punishment. Believe me, I would have done just that had I been able, but my terrible record was interpreted as one might imagine as being that of an incurable, incorrigible criminal unworthy of consideration. This is a major part of the painfully hellish trap I have referred to. I am convinced that from my earliest years as a rebellious, poorly managed, uneducated, but deeply sensitive youngster I was in protest against ill-treatment. As the realization, first with cross-dressing and then as an appreciation of gender dysphoria grew, my agony just became worse. I was like an animal trapped in a swamp. The more I protested and struggled the more deeply I became entrapped.

Fate can take many unkind turns in one's life. The unkindest cut of all was possibly the first, when my mother died. Such security as I enjoyed was totally and completely undermined and I think that with mother love, a more responsible father with stronger concern and visible affection for his children, and a climate of understanding and security I may have grown up like any other normal child. I am not suggesting that I would have been a perfect child. There would have been problems without doubt, but they would have been closer to those of the average child brought up in a secure home atmosphere. This is without regard to my underlying condition of transsexualism which would have been present in any event. That alone could have been a source of problems within the family as so frequently happens.

Suddenly with mother's death my sister and myself were unwanted baggage to be shoved around and parked wherever a bed and shelter could be found. My sister was devastated but kept her feelings repressed. Whereas I rebelled, my sister with a far more peaceful disposition stayed in line and bore the rigours and perils of being under the same roof as the hateful stepmother. She never got into trouble like I did, but the experience left her permanently scarred also.

* * * * *

I had made a serious suicide attempt in early 1969 because of severe depression over my transsexualism and the never-ending trap I seemed to be in, but I felt I did not stand a chance for treatment. I could not consider myself a man; I was a woman except for the visible genitals, and on top of it all I was being abused. I was full of tension and discomfort being in with men.

To me transsexualism comes through as a physical deformity. The experts know that the mind can never be changed but the body can be adjusted to bring it into line with the mind. Everyone with any knowledge seemed to know this except the men who ran the prisons and their medical staffs.

In any event after this failed suicide attempt I said nothing to the psychiatrists except "My only solution is death." I was certified as insane and shipped off to Riverview Mental Hospital, near New Westminster. I saw a doctor and refused to discuss my situation believing once again that it would be just another brush off. However, after about my third visit to the doctor's office he informed me that if I did not start talking I could be there for the rest of my life.

So I told him everything I could think of which had a bearing on the subject and his reply was: "No problem, you are not the only one. I'll write a letter to Dr. MacD. who will make sure you will get help." The late Dr. MacD. was the B.C. Pen psychiatrist and while I felt cheered up by this I still had lots of doubts. As it turned out Dr. MacD. did not want to deal with the issue. Instead he gave me an injection of LSD 25, which is LSD in its purest form, telling me that this would make me feel better!

It did not make me feel better. It made me feel more afraid than ever and by the time I was placed back in segregation that night, I was quite paranoid. It was difficult for me as a sensitive person to see violence and bloodshed and that night I seemed to dream of this sort of thing all through the night and even to this day it is often a recurring dream.

On the week nights we were allowed out of our cells to go to the recreation area for two hours. I rarely went out unless I was with someone with whom I could feel safe. On one such evening someone stood up and walked over to another con, grabbed him from behind, reached around with a big knife and cut his throat from ear to ear, almost it seems cutting the man's head off. The next day word got around that it was the wrong person and that someone else had been meant for execution!

On another evening we were walking back from the gym, and as we started up the stairs someone eased up behind me and tapped me on the shoulder. He motioned with his finger to his lips to move aside which I did, and as soon as his path was clear he lunged at the man ahead of me driving a knife into him about ten times. I remember I was stunned but could only move on with the crowd. Blood was running down the steps as we stepped over the fallen body. For the peaceful like myself, these sort of events were a living nightmare, but it was more than your life was worth to support any investigation. There was a code of silence if you wished to see the next day and there was no greater crime under this code than being a stool pigeon.

Then in March 1970, it was all over and I was released, hoping to never return.

* * * * *

27

Prisoner of Gender

Chapter Three

Meet My Friend Joe

A fter coming out of B.C. Pen in March 1970, I had a strong desire to visit my father, as I had only seen him on one occasion when he came to visit me during the previous two-year period.

He was happy to see me and I remember we had quite a talk. Even my stepmother was pleasant to me! My father had always wanted to see me go straight and stay away from using heroin. I found a place to live and got myself a job with Nalley's Ltd. Very shortly afterwards I ran into a girl who had lived in my old neighbourhood and I remembered she had always had a crush on me. I thought to myself, "Maybe if I could establish a relationship and have sex with a female, these inner feelings I have would go away."

She was anxious to get married, but almost from the beginning the marriage was something of a disaster. The problems all centred around our sexual relationship. I had trouble maintaining an erection and the only way in which we could enjoy any action was if I was in the underside position. Even then there was difficulty.

I would have to close my eyes and in my imagination reverse my sexual organs so that I had the vagina and breasts and she had the penis. As long as there was no interuption in this thought process I would achieve an orgasm, but 90 per cent of the time I would come back to reality part way through and then could no longer function. She would understandably become upset with me and become frustrated.

I would be left depressed and not long afterwards noticed that these inner feelings I had were so deeply rooted that they would never go away! Things had not really changed as when I had masturbated in prior years, the only way I could achieve orgasm was to visualize myself as a complete woman in my fantasy mind. I never did have a strong male libido in the first place.

About halfway through our short marriage of ten months, I told Linda, my wife, that I had always wished from my earliest recollections that I had been born female, that I identified myself as being female, and this was the reason why sex between us was no good.

For the last few months of the marriage we did not have sex together. One day she was supposed to be out for some time at a dog-grooming salon but came home early and found me in full female attire and make-up. She walked right back out of the door of our home and I never saw her again. I could not really blame her. Naturally she wanted a man, but if my mind was not even oriented in that direction, how could one expect the body to function without the mind directing it.

From there, having lost my one hope for a normal life, I drifted back to the "corner" at Main and Hastings, the centre of Vancouver's drug traffic, where I knew I would find complete acceptance. With the comfort of acceptance I did not want to leave my old friends. Very quickly I became involved in using heroin again. Euphoria induced by shooting up temporarily replaced my now deep depression following the failure of my relationship with Linda.

A couple of months later reality hit! If I stayed here using heroin I would soon be back in prison with men. Not a happy thought—in fact a deeply depressing one. I went into a dark alley, decided death would be better and plunged a knife four times deeply into my abdomen. However, because the knife was a stiletto, I did not bleed externally but it was very painful, my abdomen bulging with internal bleeding for at least an hour. Finally I called for help, and an ambulance took me to hospital.

Because I was afraid of entering a psychiatric facility once again, I said that someone had tried to rob me. Ten days in hospital followed and then it was back to the street and a resumption of heroin. Eventually I robbed a grocery store for $50 because I was going through heroin withdrawal. I was so sick from withdrawal I could not even get away from the store.

In February 1972 I was sentenced to five years and entered the B.C. Pen once again. Shortly after I was transferred to Matsqui Institution. I escaped in July 1972 and went right back to the streets again and heroin use. With disguises and good identification I managed to avoid recapture for three and a half months. During that time I ran errands, made deliveries, and helped a few people who in turn helped me, and therefore I did not have to steal or rob in order to support my heroin habit.

Picked up once again, I was returned to Matsqui and placed in the hole there for about two months and then returned to the general prison population. My shyness and sensitivity was obviously noticed and I had male prisoners coming on to me for sex. For the most part when I said "No, leave me alone" they would leave, but there were a few who continuously came back and I became very afraid of one person in particular. I started to carry a knife for self-protection. It made me feel safer, but I did not know if I could use it should it become necessary. I managed to mask my fear for if I had let it show I would be pressured all the more.

Then one weekend I was sleeping in with my door open just a crack, when this fellow of whom I had been feeling very afraid sneaked into my cell. I was lying on my stomach with the knife in my hand under the pillow. He was big and I could feel his weight almost crushing me as he jumped on top of me and tried to get under the bed covers. Somehow I managed to throw him off and as he landed on his back on the floor I jumped down on top of him and put the knife to his throat telling him to stay away from me. I could see that he was obviously shocked and frightened by my strong rejection of him. He cried out with "Please don't cut me." After that he never bothered me again.

I did have a couple of friends I could talk to who were not interested in sexually molesting me, but at the same time because of their dealing with drugs inside Matsqui Institution they could not risk siding with me when I had problems. Because they were selling heroin and cocaine they had to keep a very low profile. Had something happened and they were to become involved on my behalf with the guards, then these guys were at risk of being found with drugs and money in their possession.

I did use heroin and Valium as often as possible to help with my anxiety. Then in 1974 thirteen of us were transferred back to B.C. Pen for supposedly trafficking in drugs. A note was given to the head of security with all names attached. A lawyer got this transfer quashed within 72 hours and we were told to go back to Matsqui, or another medium-security institution of our choice.

I chose to remain in the segregation unit where I stayed for over ten months until, as earlier explained, I almost destroyed my left arm. This was due to several things, most importantly my gender dysphoria and having to live in a male institution where I was being raped and abused. There was a feeling of hopelessness and that I would never be at peace. Gradually I developed claustrophobia and could no longer cope with living in solitary confinement. Up until this point, late 1974, I had spent at least 12 years out of 16 in solitary confinement. While at Matsqui Institution between 1972 and 1974, I did manage to obtain my grade 11 equivalency, so I still had some hope of completing my education.

* * * * *

After the slashing of my arm in my futile suicide attempt, I was in hospital for about five weeks. It was here that I met Joe, who was serving an habitual criminal sentence, which amounts to natural life unless paroled.

Joe would visit me daily in the hospital and bring me tobacco and other things I needed and we had come to know each other quite well. He had a wife and children and to that point had served 12 years of his sentence, seeing the parole board once per year. He now refused to see the parole board ever again and resolved to spend the rest of his life in prison. He was a former boxer and I thought I could feel secure with him. He was well-liked by institutional staff and seemed to be able to get just about anything he wanted. He was being transferred to Mountain Institute and said that he would put in a word with the prison psychologist, a Dr. Deslaurier, so that I could transfer with him.

This is what happened and Joe and I remained together, with him treating me as the woman I have always felt myself to be. Joe knew horses very well and would bet in exhibition horse races. He always had between five and seven hundred dollars on him in ready cash. He provided money for me to get hormones brought in from outside, make-up, female underwear, sweaters, blouses and drugs. These items were brought into the institution by guards and also prisoners who had been on day or weekend passes. A transsexual I had known had given me the name of a doctor in Vancouver through whom I could get prescription hormones. From my first time in Oakalla prison in 1966 right through to my final release in 1992, there were always guards who would "pack" if the price was right.

In 1975 while I was at Mountain, Joe and myself came up with the idea of counselling young offenders at a juvenile institution about five miles away. We believed we could give good sound advice based on our experiences. I drew up a memo to Warden Walter Mort and he cleared the way for us to go unescorted once per week.

The juveniles were all ears and enthusiastic about this and it went very well for about six months and then I transferred to Ferndale Institution so that was the end of the program. Our outlook was that even if we could save and help one person then our efforts had not been in vain. If my own life had been different I think I would have enjoyed working as a counsellor.

In summer 1975 after being at Mountain for nine or ten months I was given a pass program of three days per week and two weekends per month. Now I could purchase items personally, without the extra cost. I felt so good when taking estrogen and I knew that what I really needed was sex-change surgery, but I did not know who to turn to for help.

I was encouraged by Joe to bring him whisky on a regular basis, plus his favourite cigars. Also at that time there were many heroin addicts at Mountain, so Joe would have me bring back 50 caps[1] per week which he would get someone to sell for him, doubling his money. One day he got caught with a pocket full of money and was sent back to B.C. Pen, but within two months he was back. I had decreased the amount of heroin I was using while he was away and I had given quite a bit away to addicts who were sick. When Joe got back he was very upset with me and smashed me in the face, breaking my nose. This was punishment because I had blown what money was left instead of building the stash.

---

[1] A cap or capsule contains one milligram of heroin.

The fact was I actually wanted to stop using heroin and therefore started giving it away to get it out of temptation's way. He eventually saw things my way and I continued on this pass program for about three more months. I continued to bring him his whisky and I got my hormones. I still occasionally bought heroin once he replenished his money, but I wanted away from the whole situation.

In 1976 my classification officer, Vasha Starry, asked me if I wanted to go to Ferndale Minimum Security Institution and I agreed. He was concerned about my inner feelings which I had told him about long before. He asked me if I wanted to have a discussion with Dr. Saad, the institution's psychiatrist. I was quite eager as this seemed to offer hope.

Dr. Saad came through with a disappointing response. He just brushed it all aside saying it was just a phase I was going through. This was the third psychiatric response and there was something curiously repetitive in the whole process. This business of a "phase I was going through" was like suggesting that I was still a child who might grow out of a bed-wetting problem. In truth I was a man, then 27 years of age, and even though I had a record which no one could be proud of, I had by now gone through the phases of growing up. I had bad habits and I liked to think some good ones too, but gender dysphoria was not something that one ever goes through, like witnessing an eclipse of the moon or being caught in the rain! If it is established in a person it is a generally accepted fact, among the specialist caregivers who deal with the condition, that it starts in the foetal period of one's life and invariably increases in intensity as the sufferer grows older, as I have pointed out before.

Knowing what I knew then and what is even more apparent today, I was not only a prisoner of the system in incarceration terms, but it seems that I was also hostage to the whims of doctors who did not want to be bothered. With few rights I never had the chance of dealing with someone who really had expertise. Who on the outside had to deal with a major health problem by sticking his head in a gas oven? Very few, except those bent on suicide, because on the outside they invariably had a range of options. There were always alternatives in terms of whom to consult and what form of treatment to take. But convicts simply had to do what they were directed to do, right or wrong, and hang the consequences. A thinking psychiatrist with any experience in the field of gender dysphoria would by now have drawn some directional conclusions, which would have told him the next step.

I have to wonder why some doctors put themselves on about the same level as God. References have been made to this arrogant attitude earlier, but it wasn't until 1980 that this doctor saw fit to call on other medical professionals for an opinion backed by extensive expertise. Then there was classification officer Vasha Starry. He was admittedly not a doctor, but he was a perceptive, intelligent man as he would have to be to do his job effectively. He had listened to my story, took an interest in me and recognised the genuineness of what I told him and yet it was of no account to the doctor. I am not a particularly religious person, but if there is such a thing as one day having to answer before God, there are a number of staff and their consultants in the prison system who will surely be on the carpet to explain their shortcomings.

* * * * *

Chapter Four

Life or Death

I've been thinking of writing this book since 1973, although today, over 20 years later, there is much more to unfold in my life in order to round out my story. At that point in 1973, I was so depressed, frustrated and bitterly angry with the ever present feeling that I was right and the system was very wrong in this matter of my transsexualism.

The anxiety was bad then and it felt like I could not take it anymore. I used to think how nice it would be to just live out in the forest, miles away from civilization with only a little cabin, living off the land and with the animals and birds as my neighbours. It was a matter of hiding from reality and my personal misery.

Remember that I had been a social outcast since the age of eight and with the exception of brief periods of freedom I had come to regard the criminal population as being the place where I belonged, like an alien in an alien world. When you grow up, pass through your adolescence, in my case a little like a sorcerer's apprentice, and do all your important developing into adulthood in those sort of surroundings, it is almost a foregone conclusion that it will appear more acceptable than the straight, non-criminal and good life on the outside where men and women work, gain an education, love, have children and generally prosper, and for whom a life of crime would be totally intolerable.

Readers will no doubt wonder why I did not give up heroin, which I knew to be intrinsically wrong. This is like getting an alcoholic to give up his last bottle of whisky, before it has all been drained by him. So long as it is there, it will be used and abused, and in the process will bend one's judgement and view of life. Drugs and alcohol create false values and ambitions, and while they last, even illusions of peace and tranquility, but while one travels through this world of make-believe these substances go about their insidious business of destroying you from within.

To recognise and give up something like drugs only occurs because you yourself come to certain conclusions and decide to act upon them. Expert counselling is a big help in normal circumstances, but my circumstances were never normal. My reasoning capability was always coloured by my criminal past and completely overshadowed by my ever-present gender dysphoria. Without a doubt that was and remains the most important influence in my life. While crime was the influence for the bad, gender dysphoria was an influence for the good. Had it ever been permitted to gain the upper hand in my life, and by that I mean had it been channelled to my advantage rather than to my detriment by the prison system, I think I could and would have come into and enjoyed a normal life as a sex-changed woman, doing the things I like—nothing overly ambitious, but generally letting my urge to tend to and help others have free rein.

Even in the circumstances of my imprisonment I usually had a tendency in a natural feminine sort of way to look after another person, usually my protector, and all I asked in return was some loyalty, and some of the security that his presence could create.

As recently as three months ago in terms of the evolution of this long-thought-of book, upon which I had even made a few starts, I would put it off, overcome by extreme anxiety. My co-author Stephanie, with her particular qualities, helped me focus on the book as a positive project, imparting much of her own confidence and drive. But after one month of steady writing and the open discussion between the two of us, I still suffer from the anxieties and severe headaches, as well as bad dreams which arise as I relive the past.

What keeps me buoyant in tackling this project is the belief that I have a story which deserves to be told. It is not a matter of appeasing my own ego, but perhaps of helping others caught in, or about to be enmeshed in, the same trap at some time in the future. It will do me good to get it off my chest and is one more important step in realising my ambition to complete my gender change in every sense of what is possible, together with my rehabilitation to a normalized life.

Bad dreams, as I have said, recur, and the memories which they stir give a kaleidescopic impression of much that the system is all about. There are memories which reoccur in my dreams of being strong-armed, raped or being treated like so much garbage, sick cons shoving me roughly aside so they can get their medication first. I ask, "Where do they get off thinking they are any better than anyone else?" This really burns me, but these guys were weightlifters in a hurry to get to the weight pit in order to be sure they had a bench. I wasn't about to confront them, so I'd shrug my shoulders and say "what the hell."

It happened several times so I decided that to avoid this I would just wait until the very last, discretion being the better part of valour. This is just a small example of reliving 30 years of hell!

I recall seeing someone standing by his door weakly crying for help. He had been stabbed, opening up a four-inch gash so that his intestines were hanging half-way down his thigh. I helped him to lie down on his bunk and managed to push the intestines back inside the gash and put a folded towel over top. I told him to give me two minutes to get off the range before he pushed his panic button. I didn't want to be involved at all, but I was in a cell directly across from the victim. I had witnessed the entire incident and knew the young prisoner had done nothing to warrant the attack, which made it seem worse. I instinctively had to help him, it was the humane thing to do. But to say this was an upsetting situation would be an understatement. It was hell for the victim and another hell for me. To have told what I knew as a witness would have been a matter of signing my death warrant, such is the jungle which our modern jails actually are. The knife was very rusty and the fellow remained in an oxygen tent for four months due to very severe blood poisoning.

In my dreams I see a dark spot in front of the doorway leading into my unit and I wonder what it is, but as I get very close I know that it is blood. There is so much of it that I don't know how Don (my very special friend of nine years whom I came to see as my lifetime partner) and myself are going to get into the door which is open without stepping in the blood. My adrenalin flows, I feel anxiety and I smell fear. There is a barred railing and posts about three feet out, and we manage to half throw and half swing ourselves into the doorway. The blood belongs to someone killed and drained of his blood.

There are other bloody incidents as well, over a period of 30 years. I recall sitting down in a barber chair and the person next to me was having a shave and all of a sudden everyone was splattered in blood. The prisoner's head lay hanging half decapitated down the back of the barber chair. Needless to say I had nothing done to my hair that day! I did not want to see anymore blood and turmoil.

I looked at it all in the sense that they had had my body, but I'd never let them take my mind. There was a secure feeling when locked in my cell; I could lay down and ease the muscles caused by tension and anxiety. I could finally relax.

Today when I wake in the morning I usually have to take 60 mg of codeine plus my anti-anxiety pills, due to the great deal of physical and mental pain I suffer. However, in writing this story and if I succeed in making people aware of how it was and how it still is, I will not have suffered completely in vain. Reliving all this now in thoughts and dreams is very painful but my story must be told.

* * * * *

I transferred to Ferndale Institution and continued with my pass program. I had met some people in Mission some nine months earlier when I started on this program. These were a couple, Lori and Keith, with whom I stayed occasionally as they had a spare bedroom. They loaned me an old car to get back and forth from Ferndale, which is about ten miles from downtown Mission. The three of us would chop firewood and go chicken catching, which was a messy job, in order to earn some money. They were living in the forest quite close to Stave Falls in a very peaceful setting which I found interesting and relaxing.

Lori and Keith were making plans to move to Edmonton, but in the meanwhile she picked up on something different about me. One day she commented that I was always into dishes, sweeping and dusting and doing any other household chore which caught my attention, so I told her about transsexualism. Jokingly she called me "Cinderella" and we all got along fine. About three weeks later they made their move to Edmonton and once again I was alone. However, Keith let me keep the car as they had received a new one for a wedding present, so I still had the means to travel back and forth to visit my sister in Vancouver.

This was October 1976 and with Lori and Keith gone I spent many a lonely day, walking aimlessly along the railway tracks in and around Mission, wondering constantly how I was going to raise the $7,500 I needed for surgery (a figure I was given by Candy, a transsexual friend who is now dead). She said I could go to New York and even sketched a street map to give me the location of the clinic, but failed to tell me something which I now know very well—there had to be extensive psychiatric and psychological assessment work and counselling done ahead of time. In fact, at that time there were two years of preparation, including extensive supervised hormone therapy, before I would be judged ready for surgery and to this point I had not even achieved the distinction of finding a single psychiatrist who would condescend to even give me the courtesy of a proper hearing.

Today, 17 years later and living on a disability pension, I still don't know where the money will come from. To achieve any final normalization in my life my extreme form of transsexualism requires surgery as much as many other medical conditions. This I can no more help than the fact that I was born with hazel eyes and blonde hair. During the past year B.C. Medical Plan covered surgery costs of $180,000 for an epileptic girl hoping to eradicate or at least minimise the epilepsy. Nothing improved as the result of brain surgery except that it caused her to lose the use of one of her arms.

My surgery would cost, as I have noted, up to $8,000 and would have returned me to being a whole person, but in 1986 B.C. Medical Plan embargoed any further contributions for sex reassignment surgery. To that point they had been financing two thirds of the package, but then Mr. Dueck, the health minister of the day, labelled the whole process as being "frivolous."

But reverting to 1976, the point where I am at with my story, I knew nothing of all this, the processes involved or what coverage might be available. No one can say that my frequent protestations to prison doctors and the physical injuries I inflicted upon myself were not in the record. They were the result of my protest to society that I suffered from unattended gender dypshoria. But could anyone explain or even try to understand? No one, except for a few exceptional people like Vasha Starry, mentioned in Chapter Three. I think he understood as well as any layman, but then again he had no authority to do anything beyond referring me to the prison psychiatrist, who out of sheer laziness or inability, I am not sure which, sent me back once again to the prison treadmill to put in more years of time until another break occurred. Let me repeat that my efforts were not to save time in prison, but to seek proper and adequate treatment for my genuine medical condition and at some time hopefully to be transferred to a women's prison.

While I was living in Mission I was thinking again of bank robbery. I know it sounds ridiculous, but remember I had been pretty much out of the mainstream of regular life and the only calling in which I had served a proper apprenticeship was bank robbery! I had never possessed a gun for this purpose and therefore never pulled one on a defenceless teller. It was a matter of passing a note. "Give me all the money, I have a gun" was sufficient. Someone had told me long ago to always imply that a weapon was handy and sure enough it always worked for me. I would take the money, calmly walk out so as not to draw attention, walk to my car conveniently parked nearby and then do a zig-zag course through lanes and streets to throw a pursuing cop car off the scent.

I was still living alone in Mission and was very depressed. If I did more robberies I might get caught and would certainly go back to prison. I decided that death once again would be a better answer, so I had my car tuned up and bought a full tank of gas and a bottle of whisky before heading up to Stave

Falls, driving to a lonely secluded spot in the bush. I had heard of carbon monoxide poisoning but did not know the effective way to do it. I thought so long as all the windows were tightly closed and the engine left running I would drift off into a sleep from which there would be no return. It never seemed to occur to me that the exhaust had to get inside the car! I had drunk half the whisky and fell asleep around midnight. I was surprised when I woke up at about 5 a.m. with the engine still running. I cried and felt lost and afraid in the earliest light of dawn.

Shortly after this incident I met another working couple who let me stay with them in return for looking after their two young boys. I remained very depressed and with nowhere to turn. I took a large quantity of sleeping pills hoping once again for a peaceful death, but no, I was frustrated once again when someone found me.

My thoughts returned to bank robbery and as suicide had failed on these two occasions I threw all caution to the wind, robbing four banks within a week. I had the money for surgery and with some over I bought a better car. I stopped at this couple's house to pick up a few possessions and now I was New York bound to seek my surgery.

Pious hope though it was, the whole episode was a mirage for two reasons. The first I have already recounted, i.e. the requirement for lengthy presurgical assessment and supervised hormone therapy. The other was within seconds of fulfilment.

As I stepped out of the car I heard, "Johnson, freeze, turn around and get your hands on top of the car."

Out of my left eye I caught sight of a detective holding his coat back with his left hand while his right hand rested on his gun, ready to draw for the slightest reason. As he frisked me I felt so totally drained. It was like watching the last of the bath water, symbolizing my life, draining out while I was powerless to replace the stopper. I realized soon enough that all was lost.

I was sentenced to twelve years consecutive to my preceding five-year sentence which was not quite finished. It was Christmas 1976 when I was shipped to the B.C. Pen once again to find that a good friend, Kenny B., was there on the tier below me. He called up to me and passed me a heaping tablespoon of heroin. I thanked him and asked him who all this was for. He merely replied "enjoy."

It lasted about a week and during that period I relaxed and planned an escape. Back in B.C. Pen maximum security I could no longer get my unprescribed hormones! I went through many changes, both emotional and physical and no more than barely tolerable depression.

I remained in B.C. Pen for about a year, spending most of the time in segregation, and then was transferred back to Mountain Prison, again to be back with Joe, my old friend who was familiar with all the prison rackets. I knew I would get away and about six months later Joe paid off a guard to take me out on a pass. I ran and robbed a bank, but was caught within an hour and was sentenced to another four years consecutive in 1978. Again I was returned to B.C. Pen.

All told I had now accumulated sentences including those for escape of 23 years and I was still only 29. I felt totally lost. I had no hope of living happily. I didn't know what to do as I stood in front of the mirror, a shoelace tied tightly around my neck. I looked at myself in the mirror. I knew what I wanted, I knew what I needed and this was not the way to achieve either. I don't know how many times I loosened and tightened the shoelace, until I finally put the blade to my jugular vein. Then with so much strength I sliced the jugular in half. This was it, I didn't want to live anymore and certainly not in a man's prison. In my heart and mind I was a woman and if only the system had been flexible enough to handle this I could have spared both it and myself a great deal of expensive dangerous trouble.

I let the blood shoot over into the back of the cell and into the toilet so as to avoid drawing attention. I then sat on the edge of the bed by which time the heaviest flow was over but I did manage to curl up on my bunk in the foetal position. I felt very warm and thought to myself, "Finally I will have peace."

A prisoner delivering newspapers walked by and spotted me. I could hear him talking and calling a guard, but I felt safe that I was too far gone to be saved yet again. By now I could not open an eye or move a finger. The whole episode ended on a strange note. It was another half hour before I reached Royal Columbian Hospital in New Westminster and yet I lived. One wonder's how this could have been possible?

It was about a week before I regained consciousness and eventually saw the new psychiatrist, Dr. Multhanna. I told him about the ever-present transsexualism and he talked to Dr. Saad, psychiatrist at the Regional Psychiatric Centre which was under the authority of Correctional Services Canada. Dr. Saad assured me that he would look for specialists in transsexual medicine in order for me to be assessed by them.

About one year later, constantly depressed and having heard nothing further about specialists, who clearly existed because others had received treatment in Canada, including Candy whom I referred to earlier, I once again took matters into my own hands. This time I castrated myself. I wanted to stop erections and eliminate the natural flow of testosterone which to me appeared to be the culprit in the aggression and irrationality I had showed over most of my life.

I went about it in a methodical way to be sure there would be no possibility that I would die this time. This was in no way a suicide attempt, but I had to get someone's meaningful attention. I did the deed with the aid of a suitable tourniquet, a knife which I had managed to sterilise and then with surgical precision carefully cut through the scrotum from bottom to top. I got dressed having used a towel folded and worn through and under the crotch to absorb blood, and then walked to the front of the range and flushed the two testicles down the toilet, thinking to myself that I did not want prison staff to find them and try to reattach them in some way!

It was only then that I felt secure as I walked to the nursing station and told the duty nurse of my deed.

* * * * *

Prisoner of Gender

Chapter Five

Self-Surgery is Not Recommended

When I reached the nursing station I calmly stated to the nurse in charge that I needed an ambulance to take me to the outside hospital to be stitched up. She became very concerned as I told her that I had castrated myself. It was instant panic for the nurses, regardless of the fact that I assured them that there was no need for panic because I was bleeding very little. I had applied a very tight tourniquet and was feeling no pain and losing very little blood, perhaps half a pint all told.

The nurses ushered me back to my cell and had me lay down on the bed, to see exactly what I had done. Shortly after, I was whisked away to hospital where the tubes were cauterized and I was stitched up. I was held there for about a week before being transferred back to the institution hospital.

It seems at this point that the psychiatrist, Dr. Saad, became very concerned and took my case seriously, because within about six months I had my first interview of a series with Dr. D.B. Watson, a psychiatrist, and also with Ms. Pat Diewold, a registered clinical psychologist. Both were well-known as specialists in gender dysphoria cases and soon after both became founding members of the Vancouver Hospital Gender Dysphoria Clinic.

Dr. Watson's psychiatric report and Ms. Diewold's back-up psychological assessment confirmed very clearly that I was transsexual. These reports (referred to from hereon as the

Watson/Diewold report) constitute a most important document which I obtained through the Freedom of Information Act. They are quoted in full in Chapter 13.

One should remember these reports were ordered by the Regional Psychiatric Centre psychiatrist, Dr. Saad, to whom they were submitted in June 1980. Despite the fact that Dr. Watson recommended I be placed on female hormone therapy, the institution physician in charge of prescriptions refused to prescribe! This was in spite of the superior knowledge of specialists. I was frustrated by the negative action of a man of far lesser knowledge and little experience, if any, in dealing with gender dysphoria. Bob Dylan said, "Where your head is, is your life." A very true statement. Indeed, my life was circumscribed by the workings of my mind and if any outside agency sought to change my transsexualism by means of neglect, abuse or ongoing punishment, it was simply not going to happen. Transsexualism in any individual simply does not work that way. Outside efforts to obliterate it simply drive it in deeper.

During my stay at Regional Psychiatric Centre I occupied much of my time doing embroidery and needlepoint pictures. While here also I had somehow become aware of a Toronto-based group, FACT (Foundation for Advancement of Canadian Transsexuals). The director of FACT sent me much information and we wrote back and forth for a lengthy period of time. I was told that OHIP (Ontario Hospital Insurance Plan) covered the major cost of sex-reassignment surgery so I made a hasty decision and asked Correction Services Canada to transfer me to the Ontario region. Since the assessment on me was completed there remained no reason to keep me at Regional Psychiatric Centre and I was transferred to Kent Maximum Security Institution at Agassiz, B.C., where I stayed in segregation for six months until the transfer to Ontario came into effect in December 1980. Again despite the fact that the Watson/Diewold report travelled with my other medical records, the prison doctor at Kent again refused to prescribe female hormones!

This did not make sense then and still does not to this day. Correctional Services asked for the assessment from specialists and yet they refused to implement the recommendations! There can be no defence for this. If they knew more than the experts why did they use experts to make assessments for them? Maybe they hoped to only hear things from the experts which supported their idea of the *status quo*. If a family doctor sent a patient to a specialist for cancer or tuberculosis, for example, and then just plainly refused to act on the specialist's recommendations, would he not be brought up for professional malpractice? Unless he had a powerful and justifiable reason I am sure he would have been on the carpet. There were times when the world around me seemed to have gone entirely mad, and Corrections Service Canada in the form of its own doctors was the maddest of all!

When I reached Ontario I was placed in Joyceville Medium Security Institution, and there I found another transsexual called Heather, so at least I had someone to talk to who had an understanding.

Dr. Webb, the prison doctor, was very ignorant. It seems that he lacked knowledge of endocrine medicine and any form of compassion or humanity. He offered me replacement hormone therapy in the form of the male sex hormone testosterone. If I wanted male hormones I would not have castrated myself! Heather had breasts which were shrinking because she could not get her hormones from this doctor either. I became so angry with him that I told him off and slammed his door quite violently. I started walking down the stairs but was so upset, I walked back to his office and kicked his door in, smashing the door window which was half the area of the door. Had I not gone through hellfire and brimstone to demonstrate that I wanted to be free of masculine features? I waved my finger at him and said I'd see him in court. I was immediately taken to the hole where I found a razor blade and attempted to sever my penis. It was very painful and I moaned loudly. I did not deliberately want to suffer, I wanted help!

Once again I was taken to an outside hospital for stitching and from there directly to Regional Psychiatric Centre, Ontario. The doctors there would do nothing for me, so I made several more attempts to remove the penis. I was told that the assessments from B.C. doctors meant nothing in Ontario and that I would have to be assessed by the province's own gender dysphoria clinic, the Clarke Institute of Psychiatry in Toronto.

In 1981 clinic staff headed by Dr. B. Steiner came to interview me at R.P.C. They agreed with the Watson/Diewold report from Vancouver confirming yet again that they diagnosed transsexualism and that I should be placed on female hormone therapy. Once again the mad hatter's tea party went into gear, and once again the general practitioner in charge of prescribing refused to act on their recommendations.

I then wrote to Dr. D. Craigen, Director General of Health Care for Corrections Service Canada who wrote back stating that there was no policy for treatment of transsexuals and that I would have to wait until I was released.

Meanwhile I had been interviewed by the parole board and was told by the senior member, Max Steinburg, that "I will not authorize any type of release plan until you are back on hormones and in a better frame of mind."

This was a true Catch 22 situation. I could not obtain parole until I was back on hormones and I could not get hormones because there was no policy. Policy or not, Dr. Webb had offered me male hormones in possibly the most idiotic gesture I was ever to receive from any doctor in my lifetime! What it demonstrated was that by any standard known in treating transsexualism this was about tantamount to offering a would-be suicide a loaded gun with which to protect himself!

Finally I wrote to Hon. Robert Kaplan, Solicitor General of Canada, because Corrections Service came under him in this capacity. This was 1981 and the Trudeau government was still in power. In my letter I described my dilemma. I was trapped in a jungle of bureaucratic immobility. I sent him a copy of the letter from the parole board along with that from Dr. Craigen. Mr. Kaplan became my saviour. With his reply he enclosed a copy of his letter to Dr. Craigen.

He told Craigen, "If you have transsexuals in prison, then there must be a policy formulated in regard to the treatment of transsexuals."

When I received this letter so much anxiety seemed to drain out of me. After all, Dr. Craigen could not refuse the Hon. Robert Kaplan; but true to form, the prison bureaucratic wheel turned at glacial speed. It was not until 13 months later that a vague policy was announced.

I think it was late 1982 when I finally started receiving female hormones, and in no time was feeling very much better. But bureaucratic protest was not over. Normally I would have been returned to Joyceville. However, Dr. Webb stated that he would not be responsible for me and did not want me in Joyceville. So I was then sent to Millhaven Maximum Security Institution and the officials there wanted to keep me locked up in the segregation unit. They said my presence would otherwise cause trouble in the main prison population.

Thirteen years of solitary confinement had caused me to become quite claustrophobic, and they could not hold me in segregation without proper cause or against my wishes. As I came into the main population I was swarmed by men and it was very disturbing for me. However, I did know a few of the prisoners and they watched over me. A big guy by the name of

Garry, who was serving a 25-year life term before possible parole, took an interest in me and we became friends. Despite his sentence he smiled a lot and always tried to cheer me up when he would see me depressed.

Garry looked after me and we remained together for about six months, until he was finally granted a new trial. It was not likely he would be back because I had read the transcripts from his first trial and he was clearly innocent. The second trial freed him. However, before leaving Millhaven he asked Cliff to look after me. Cliff was a very powerful man and I felt safe with him since I had come to know him quite well, as he was a good friend of Garry's.

Shortly after a particularly vicious Frenchman (the one who had stabbed the young fellow leaving him with his intestines hanging out, whom I mentioned earlier) was making advances towards me when Cliff was not around. I did not entice him in any way, telling him I was not interested in him and making it clear that I was with Cliff and wanted to keep it that way. Regardless, his approaches continued.

One night Cliff and I were in my cell at opposite sides of the bed, playing gin rummy on a board situated between us. Without warning the door flew open and four guys appeared. Three entered the cell, one had a baseball bat, another a weight lifting bar, and the third a shank (knife). The fourth "kept point," watching for guards from the door. I was terrified and crouched in the corner. Cliff, being super strong, grabbed the locker and steered it around in front of himself trying to provide protection. He was smashed many times with the steel bar, stabbed several times in the face, and the baseball bat split his head open, exposing the bare bone of his skull.

Cliff managed to get hold of the bat and chased them out of the cell and halfway down the range screaming, "Don't come back!" My cell was covered in blood and major injury had been done to Cliff. We were both in a state of shock. The guards made a walk down the ranges every hour, and when they looked into my cell they were freaked by what they saw.

Cliff told them to go away, and that he was staying with me until the final night lock-up, so they left us alone. I had his head wrapped in several towels and taped gauze over the stab wounds to his face. He had a broken elbow and a broken leg from the weight bar. He stayed with me until final lockup and then went to the hospital for attention. I spent all night cleaning up the mess, wiping almost the entire walls down of splattered blood, placing a big pile of bloodied sheets, blankets, towels and clothes by the door. In the morning I took it all to the laundry and drew clean stuff.

Of course I was taken up to the front offices for questioning, but I could not say who the attackers were. Had I mentioned their names, which I knew well enough, it would have been a death sentence for me. The next day the Frenchman came to my cell and put a chunk of hashish on my desk and said it was for me if I would give him oral sex. I was very angry with him and told him I wanted nothing to do with him and never would. He was quite persistent but finally he left.

Cliff came out of the hospital a week later and then once again the Frenchman had the gall to appear, as Cliff and I were sitting in the servery having a coffee. He showed Cliff a big knife which was hidden under his shirt. He then told Cliff he had a lot of nerve for coming back and would die for sure if he didn't check into protective custody. Cliff and I debated the situation and then Cliff checked in. He only had a short while left to serve and I doubted I would be killed. Besides, with Cliff on crutches and with his arm in a sling, there would be no way he could protect himself so protective custody was the best thing for him.

Next day the Head of Security (CX8) came to see me and asked if I wanted segregation, since Cliff was no longer around. I appreciated his concern but I was sure I would be fine as there were other friends of Garry whom I talked and walked with in the yard, and a couple of them were pretty big men with whom I felt safe. I continued with my job in the servery and one day while I was waiting for the guard to unlock the door to the servery, a big weightlifter who had a history of strong arming for sex stood very close to me trying to maul me. I told him I was off limits and to stay away from me. Just then two heavies came and asked if this guy was bothering me. I assured them it was okay. We were just talking and then I walked away with these two guys. I then told them about this guy trying to maul me and wanting me to come to his cell. I thought that by telling them that they would watch out for me a little closer. That night as I was crossing through the gym to go outside for some fresh air I spotted two guys wearing ski masks and holding weight bars. I pretended not to notice them and just kept on and out into the prison yard.

Two hours later I walked back into the gym. I found this weightlifting strong-armer laying in the middle of the gym, his face and much of his body smashed up badly. There was a circle of blood around his head and upper body five feet in diameter. He had taken a terrible mauling probably at the hands of the two ski-masked individuals I had noticed earlier.

After Cliff left I started associating with Moose. Although well-liked, Moose was a loner and spent most of his time in his cell. He was known to make excellent moonshine and lived on the same range as me. I felt a need to alleviate some of my anxiety so asked him for a drink. I knew I would be safe with him as he invited me in. We had a couple of drinks and played some crib. This we did quite often. The Frenchman started coming on to me again quite viciously and I just didn't know what to do. Moose didn't want sex, but said to stick close to him.

Moose was killed on December 25, 1982. I became increasingly terrified with all the violence around me and the fact that I was in a male prison and not even permitted a housecoat for my privacy to and from the showers. I'd have to wrap a blanket around me. I was in a trap from which there seemed no escape. There was another Frenchman who would always give a smile and a polite "hello." He came to me one day and gently asked me if I wanted him to look after me. I felt so overwhelmed at what had been happening that I cuddled into his arms and cried. We were left alone for two months until finally one day, while my back was turned and he was bent over tying his shoelaces a steel rod was plunged into his back.

A couple of days later the warden called me to his office, and told me he didn't want me in Millhaven any longer, as I was "directly responsible" for all the bloodshed and death. It was grossly wrong to label me directly responsible, although I did not doubt that my presence was clearly disturbing to many of the men. I could have told him that when I moved in, but it was a matter of spending my entire time in segregation or finding some human company.

Once again the system demonstrated that it was totally imprisoned by its hidebound bureaucracy. A man was severely injured in what could have been murder in Cliff's case. Another man had a rod driven into his back. The men who had done these dastardly acts were the lowest of the low and should not have been allowed the freedom to commit such acts and seemingly always get away with it. The prison system could evidently overlook what amounted to a reign of terror, knowing full well that so long as I could be intimidated I could not give out names for fear of my own life. Instead I got the blame for creating temptation!

A Warrant of Committal executed on judicial order directs a peace officer to "keep the prisoner there safely" or words to that effect. That's a tall order. The prison system seems incapable of providing safe ongoing security to prisoners and to place the blame for the foregoing events I have just described on a defenceless prisoner would be a joke if it was not so unjust and pathetically inaccurate.

* * * * *

Chapter Six

The Hell of Joyceville and Millhaven

The warden had a letter on his desk from Max Steinburg of the Parole Service, Kingston. It stated that if I would agree to transfer to Joyceville again I would be guaranteed a pass program. I agreed to that and I was escorted to my cell to pack my belongings. I was then placed in a cell in the prison hospital, where a day prior someone had slashed up in that cell.

After all the blood I'd seen, I told the guard that this was too much to cope with. Blood stains were everywhere; on the mattress, pillow, walls, floor, sink and toilet. I was told to shut up and live with it. I asked for a bucket of water and a rag to clean it up, but this was refused. I called him back and said I would smash the security camera, worth about $2,000, if he didn't give me a bucket of water and rag. He told me to go ahead but I would pay for it. I then noticed the roll of toilet paper so with water from the sink I proceeded to do what I could to clean things up. Needless to say it was a terrible night trying to sleep in that slaughterhouse, for that's what it looked like.

The next day I was transferred to Joyceville and after about a month I had an interview with Beth Stacey of the Elizabeth Fry Society. She wanted to get me out on full parole right away and I would be allowed to live at the women's halfway house until I was ready and able to get a place of my own.

She came to my parole hearing, told the board her plan for me and the board agreed. I was totally shocked but very happy at the prospect. Heather had been released while I was in Millhaven and she also was living at the women's halfway house. When I got there I felt such relief. It was there that I learned there were female-to-male transsexuals as well! One was well ahead on treatment with beard and hairy chest. They both wanted to be in male halfway houses. The women there accepted me completely and we all got along fine.

Four days later I ran into someone I had met in Joyceville and he and his girlfriend invited me to their apartment for supper. After supper this fellow poured large drinks of Jack Daniels and the three of us sat on the patio talking and drinking. I asked if they would drive me back to the halfway house. Being the least affected by the drink, she drove, while I was half out of it, slouched in the back seat. All of a sudden the car stopped as Tommy wanted to get a pack of cigarettes. I called out for him to get me a pack also. Little did I know, that was not his plan. I heard running and the back door of the car opened and he dived to the floor, a gun in one hand and a money bag in the other. Without my knowledge I had once again been compromised. Had I any clue, I would have walked. I was starting to enjoy life a little and now I needed this like a hole in the head.

Caught instantly because the police were right there, I told him to say that I was just a hitchhiker, but no, he wanted to plead not guilty all the way. All three of us were charged and in the end it was another three years consecutive. I was devastated. Always a loser it seems. Everything good in my life turned to dust on every occasion. In my brushes with the law in the past I had brought on my own troubles, but for once being totally innocent I still could not keep away from trouble. All in all from February 1972 to the summer of 1983, I had managed to accumulate 26 1/2 years of sentences. Not a record to be proud of considering that I was still only 34 years old!

When I was arrested I was placed in the women's section until the next day when I asked for a razor. The matron asked me why and I touched my face and said that I could feel a slight stubble. She ran for the keeper and he asked me if I had a penis. When I told him yes, he ordered me to the men's lockup. There were young fellows there who started being sarcastic and I felt very angry.

I asked to be locked in a cell by myself, got a razor, tied a tourniquet very tightly against the pubic bone and I made a deep strong cut. My penis was now connected by a thread of skin and I was in so much pain no sound came from my throat. Later I remember saying "No penis now, put me in with the women." I passed out as they took me to hospital where they stitched the member back on. Perhaps it was well I did not lose it, as I later found out that all the penile tissue is needed for gender reassignment surgery.

When I awoke I found that I was in the Napanee Psychiatric Hospital just outside Kingston, Ont. I was interviewed by Dr. S.G. Laverty and Dr. Venita, who were psychiatrists. They thought perhaps they could help me and I agreed to have a meeting with them, another psychiatrist and four psychologists. I told them my complete life story to date. They had many questions for me and what seemed to be a very lengthy session gave me a feeling perhaps that I'd get my surgery dealt with. To quote just part of the recommendation which Dr. Laverty directed to Corrections Service Canada:

> . . . *arrangements be made to transfer Kathy Johnson to a forensic facility for further assessment with surgery as a definite objective to be considered. . . . Further rehabilitation would presumably be much easier after his sex change has been made.*

Keep in mind that this was the constructive end result of the deliberations of a committee of some seven specialists as recounted above, but once again this initiative was ignored! I returned to Regional Psychiatric for a short period, but I wanted out and a return to Joyceville. There was nothing RPC would do for me except to play with my mind and not give me my prescribed hormones for two weeks. Even when I got back to Joyceville the doctor played games and I think it was about another week before I got back on my regular dosage.

This tampering with hormones throws the emotions into a turmoil along with adverse physical affects. In 1981 it was stated by Dr. Steiner of the Clarke Institute of Psychiatry, Toronto, that I should see an endocrinologist (a specialist in the hormonal functions of the body) for blood tests and an examination which normally would then allow for periodic adjustments in hormone dosage. I saw an endocrinologist only once, prior to my release in January 1992.

Many times I would have to walk through the inner yard at Joyceville when there were 200-300 men in the yard. I would set my path, having to walk right through the middle with my head held high conveying an appearance of outer calm, but inside I trembled in fear.

Skin frisks by male guards created another difficult situation for me to face. Whenever a stabbing took place or sometimes just a routine need for a cell search and skin frisk for contraband, I would have to go through this. I didn't want to be naked and on display in front of strange men. Most of the guards liked me and didn't bother me. So many times I would say "Okay, just one guard" and they'd agree.

One warden at Joyceville said to call for him and just refuse to strip. When he would get there he'd take me to the hospital and I could strip with a nurse. Later as many female guards became employed, they didn't mind looking after the frisking. When guards would search cells sometimes they would take make-up, blouses and underwear. Within days I would have all new stuff again. Some guards were very sympathetic and I might add quite well-informed on transsexualism, which proves that ignorance was not universal among the guards at least. Sometimes they thought nothing of spending $20 out of their own pockets for some small thing to help me feel content and give me some happiness.

Guys would continue to tease, name-call and become aggressive. I was very bitter at them and the whole system and I started giving them the finger, or more often I just ignored them and they started to say "Here comes the icicle!"

In 1984 things got much worse. The vicious Frenchman and several of his friends were arriving at Joyceville. Sometimes I had a knife to my throat, sometimes threats, and I was forced to perform sex very much against my will and despite my protests. There was no escape. Garry came into Joyceville again with a new two-year sentence, together with Bobby and Bobby's nephew. Garry and I were right back together and life was bearable for a while until one evening when Garry came back to the range in a very drunken and hostile state.

I was standing at the end of the bed with my back to the door. He was wearing his heavy work boots and kicked me with the flat of the boot in my lower spine throwing me onto the bed. I was in a lot of pain and could barely move, but I did manage to get up and lock my door. The next day Garry was all over me, hugging and kissing and saying how sorry he was. What he had done created damage to my spine which I have to this day. This and other abuses while in prison have left me with three injured vertebrae and a permanently weak back.

This, however, was not the only damage to my back. A big guy who obviously didn't like my presence shoved me down a 60 degree staircase. Luckily I didn't fall far before I was able to grasp the hand railing, but this did not stop him from jumping and kicking several times on my back in an effort to dislodge me. Needless to say with roughly 220 lbs. to back the force he applied it did much further damage.

Today, I live in a small bachelor suite with constant pain as my companion. I usually need to take six Tylenol #3 daily—two at a time with each pill containing 30 mg of codeine. I also take a strong tranquilizer every four hours due to the brain damage suffered when I cut my jugular in my suicide attempt.

Garry would only have to serve a year and I badly wanted him out of my life. Garry and Bobby were getting large quantities of hashish into the institution and I was ordered to sell it, yet I did not want to be around all the guys. I was always uncomfortable and afraid. Joyceville held approximately 650 inmates and it was scary walking through a large mass of men.

I ended up sitting by the hobby shop where there was usually a guard present and I would have someone else sell the hash (about three ounces per week). Someone I could trust would pick up money, bring it to me and I'd give him the amount of hash purchased. At the end of each day the runner would have a nice piece for himself. Then for about three months there was speed to sell along with the hash. It was quite crazy, and if I had been caught with drugs I would only earn more time.

Finally Garry was gone in mid-1985. I stayed home in my cell for much of the time, usually going out only for medication, cigarettes or coffee. The Frenchman would catch me once in a while and I would be raped and he'd try to get me to service his friends. I'd cry "no" and he would slap me around. At one time he and his best friend had me trapped in a locked bathroom and they both raped me anally. If I had yelled for the guard, I would have been killed for the Frenchman would kill without conscience and for very little cause.

One day I was standing by the shuffle board waiting for the purchasing office to open. A young fellow came up to me and smashed me with his fist, perhaps 30-40 times, for no specific reason. He clearly did not like me and probably justified his action on the basis that tranny-bashing was acceptable on the same basis as gay-bashing. My head was spinning and my knees buckling. I remember thinking that if I fell, very possibly my life might be over. A friend just happened to come along and jumped between us and without further ado the young punk ran. It was a murderous and totally unjustified attack, but as usual there were no repercussions.

It was shortly after that I met Don who was a real gentleman. One day he came over to me and said he had had his eye on me for a long time and wanted to spend some time with me! He never even mentioned sex. He just wanted to go walking in the yard, lots of talking and playing cards.

Around 1986 a lot of young guys started coming into Joyceville and the level of violence increased. One day Don and I were standing outside our unit door for a little fresh air, when all of a sudden we saw three young cons attacking another young fellow. He was stabbed many times but still managed to run into his unit office and fall dead at the feet of the guards. His "crime" was that he owed a carton of cigarettes for a hit of LSD which he had bought "on the cuff," and then found that he couldn't get the carton. A senseless death, but the in-jail drug distribution was merciless; you paid your debts one way or another.

Then one morning someone Don worked with was looking for his hairbrush. He walked into the common room where people ate and sat around at tables watching television. He spotted his hairbrush lying in front of a young fellow. He asked for its return and the guy ran a blade long enough to qualify as a sword through his heart! Usually the smallest knives packed were about 12 inches long and two inches wide and well-sharpened. When I cleaned the range and bathroom I was always coming across them and I would shudder.

It was about this time, 1985-86, that there were six transsexuals in Joyceville and we wanted to start a group and have a group time allotted to us as with other groups in the prison, such as lifers, the Chinese group, 7-steps AA, John Howard and quite a few others. We were called a minority and could not have a group of our own, even though there were a couple of groups with as few as five or six members. The more we argued about it the more we were harassed by staff. If we caused too much static about something the guards would raid our cells and take everything feminine.

In the summer of '86 or '87 I wanted to get some sun on my upper body. Don and I went to a very secluded spot out in the yard, and I took my top off with him sitting up and keeping an eye out for other prisoners. I managed to get about half an hour of sun before a guard in a perimeter tower spotted me and screamed over the loudspeaker, "Johnson get your top on, or you're going to the hole!" This was because I had visible breasts. Meanwhile all through the years when I had asked for something not usual to the guys, such as a housecoat in aid of modesty it was refused. If as transsexuals we wanted to buy something like make-up or panties we were usually told, "You are in a male institution and you'll be treated as males." Oddly though, men could take their tops off; in this regard they insisted on treating us as women! It was impossible to ever win in the system.

Every transsexual in prison was abused, raped, verbally assaulted and subjected to continual harassment. One, Crystal Morgan Furry, was killed in prison. Another was Jill, whose tragedy I witnessed while in Joyceville. Jill was a friend and fellow transsexual, who couldn't get any help from the doctors. She came to me looking for tranquilizers or at least something to relax her. She was crying and very upset, but I had nothing which would have helped her. Next thing I knew she was carrying a stack of newspapers back to her cell, but I didn't immediately realize the significance of this. She hadn't mentioned suicide to me, but very shortly after everything was black with smoke. She had locked her door, torched her cell and then hung herself from the bar in the clothes closet.

If there were any repercussions from this tragedy I have no idea what they might have been. Had it have happened anywhere else within society it would have made headlines. Prison suicides are relatively common and seem to stir up as much response in the public eye as happens when a cat is run over on the road. The reason for this is that the public seldom knows anything about such events or their circumstances. There appears to be a minimum of accountability within the system and who can argue when say a relative receives a communication from the prison hierarchy to the effect that their loved one has died in prison from whatever cause. The probable response will likely be that there were no witnesses as to what actually happened for as we have seen the prison code of silence seems beyond penetration.

Don and I had decided that we wanted to be together even out in society and then after my surgery we'd settle down and have a much happier and contented life together. Don loved me very much and when he came back to the range from work he would hug me and tell me how much I meant to him. We would lay on top of the bed, cuddled together, watching TV and feeling content. His main concern was just to look after me the best he could and I loved him so much in return. He was the first man who loved me for who I am without pestering me for sex. We were together for almost eight years, six inside and the remainder outside in society until his death in August 1993.

I was being asked about parole in late 1987. The Elizabeth Fry Society in Hamilton, Ontario, was willing to accept me. First I was to go out on six weekend passes and then receive day parole to their house in June, 1988. Don was happy for me that I would be away from the anguish that prison caused me, but as we shall see this new-found freedom was yet again to turn to bitter dust.

* * * * *

Chapter Seven

Release From Purgatory

To this point I have not mentioned how I became involved with the Elizabeth Fry Society of Hamilton. I had developed a friendship with Don's sister through correspondence and by telephone. She lived in Burlington, Ont., located between Toronto and Hamilton. I therefore had some associations in the area which encouraged me to settle there even though I was from B.C. where my sister was located. At this time in 1987 I had a different classification officer and as we planned my parole she insisted that I must apply only to male halfway houses, despite the fact that I had made knowledge available to her with regard to transsexualism and also that I had been accepted by Elizabeth Fry of Kingston in 1983. It seemed to me that she felt intimidated or challenged by me.

So from there I proceeded to apply to two men's halfway houses in Hamilton, neither of which would accept me, stating that they felt my presence would disrupt the house, and on previous experience this was so. I then applied to one in Brantford and received the same result. I did not apply to any in Toronto as I did not wish to live in such a big city.

There was nowhere else for me to apply, so on my own initiative I wrote a lengthy letter with enclosed medical reports to the Elizabeth Fry Society in Hamilton. I received total acceptance from the director of Elizabeth Fry and from its director of socialization, Barbara Hill, both of whom came to see me. They drove to Joyceville Institution to interview me and right on the spot signified their acceptance of me. Barb Hill was to be my parole supervisor for 15 months.

Judy Davis Young, my classification officer who had been so insistent that I could only apply to male facilities, came down a notch or two after that and started to see matters more from my point of view. This was another example of the system's mindset and insistence on forcing the prisoner to conform to its rigid ideas in the face of all evidence to the contrary.

The six passes were to be one per month from Friday morning until Sunday midnight. The Admissions and Discharge department, which looked after all clothing, passes and releases, etc., would not allow me to leave the institution in female attire. The make-up was fine by them, but the clothing was a dead issue and this was a position they took right up to the warden level. Why one without the other is a good question, which if followed through all the time would only be the source of trouble. If you purport to be a woman it is far better to play the role completely as it is an issue of personal security. We know all about the vulnerability of women, but someone who is in between is in even greater danger.

This was totally ridiculous and another example of the half and half routine so typical of the system. When in a men's institution I had to conform to the male standards, and yet when I took my shirt off in a quiet corner of the yard to get a little sun, the guard told me to put my shirt on again or face a spell in the hole, if the reader will recall. Even two paragraphs back I described the matter of Ms. Young, my classification officer, insisting that I apply to male halfway houses, a matter of forcing a square peg into a round hole. When stepping outside the prison they must have known that I would immediately revert to living as a woman. God knows, I had been screaming and protesting about it for years, but it seems that perpetual stupidity reigned supreme at every level.

I proceeded to take the matter up with the Commissioner of Penitentiaries. Again a negative response led me to think of a way. I could leave in my track outfit, carrying my suitcase with a change of clothes, change at the Elizabeth Fry house and then reverse the process coming back. This was really a needless aggravation and just another pinprick in a long history which increased my bitterness towards Corrections Service Canada.

In my view this clothing issue and many other similar such treatments such as removing all our female things on the slightest provocation were direct contraventions of the provisions of the Canadian Charter of Rights and Freedoms, Section 12: "Everyone has the right not to be subjected to any cruel and unusual treatment or punishment." At this point the reader may think I am quibbling over something very insignificant and superficial, but in the mind of the transsexual person situations such as these are highly emotional, deeply disturbing issues and the truth of the matter is that they frequently are health-disturbing. Effectively, I was being punished for being transsexual which is not a crime in any criminal code in the Western world. The underlying and real reason for my presence in prison seemed to fade into insignificance.

My co-author expresses it well in her book *Feelings* when she talks about the transsexual's need for normalization in her life coupled with peace of mind being the ultimate and only objectives. This involves the transsexual's deep need to live and be accepted as the woman she believes she was meant to be, but for the mistake of nature. This being the case it is perfectly natural that clothes and make-up represent a part of the normalization process. After all, to a woman they are usually an expression of how she feels about herself. Clothes and make-up are outward expressions; it is also what is inside, the combination of instincts, emotions and perceptions which add up to distinguish the woman from the man.

If, as a transsexual, one has these womanly feelings, would it not be totally unnatural to expect a self-respecting woman to go around all day wearing the clothes of a man usually engaged in working on a garbage truck or in the sewers? To force a woman to do this would amount to "cruel and unusual treatment," and any self-respecting woman would immediately rebel against it. The fact that the only remaining physical feature of my former masculinity is a penis which I would happily see removed is not a very good reason for the imposition of the many cruelties within the prison system which I endured at the hands of both prisoners and prison staff. Once again even in the parole process we see evidence of a total refusal and incapability of the system to adjust rules to fit a clear set of circumstances.

I could and would ask politely for consideration and when rejected, especially when I was right, I would start demanding and when told to shut up I would have to do just that. If I rocked the boat too much orders would be given and the guards would tear my cell apart taking everything in sight right down to my plants, which were one of the few sources of pleasure I had living in a male joint.

If I put in a complaint against a particular guard then all his buddies would come down on me too. This happened to me once in 1990 or 1991. This particular guard was always harassing me, and talking crudely and lewdly, a performance which had gone on since around 1983. I bore it without complaint until 1991 when it finally got to me and I laid a complaint. He laughed it off as "just kidding." Senior Security ordered the guard to apologise to me, as if this was going to change anything. I wanted him transferred to a different range away from me, but after his light wrist slap from up high, that was not to be and he remained around to continue his harassment which he pursued with renewed vigour.

My first arrival at the halfway house for women took place with the feeling I was going to be okay and I could relax. There was no feeling of tension in the air as was always the case when I was in a group of men. There were twelve women at the house with myself making up the thirteenth. Most of these women were from Kingston where Shelley Ball, who had undergone sex reassignment surgery, was serving a life sentence. Due to their knowledge of this fact Elizabeth Fry had a full understanding of transsexualism and it greeted me with open arms.

With regard to Shelley Ball it could be noted that an outside psychiatrist and the sentencing judge recommended that Correctional Services provide Shelley with surgery so that she could serve her sentence in a women's prison. This was done in 1979 but was a good example of extreme inconsistency. One wonders why her, while the rest of the small population of prison transsexuals were consistently refused meaningful assistance even with hormones? The reason given, as I understand it, for not providing similar facilities for other transsexuals relates to a legal action that Ball brought against Corrections Canada, the exact details of which have no bearing on my case, beyond noting that 1979 was during the period when I was fighting for some sort of tangible recognition of my situation.

On my first pass I shared a room with Lori and Heather (a different Heather from the one mentioned earlier). We lay in our beds and talked and laughed before going to sleep and it all felt completely natural to me. I remained friends with these two women long after they moved out of the halfway house. I often babysat Lori's daughter and was Heather's bridesmaid one year later. Being a bridesmaid was a very special moment for me to say the least!

The passes all went well and I was feeling emotionally strong. Everyone hugged good morning as we came down for coffee in our housecoats and slippers. Women have that special facility for natural communication which made me feel so completely at ease and secure. It was the same at night and when coming in for the day.

Coming back to Joyceville at the end of each pass was like returning to the lion's den. Three days of peace with women and 27 of tension and anxiety while living with men. It was like the contrast between heaven and hell. I had six months of this routine which poses the question, if I could live contentedly in a women's halfway house why could I not live in a female prison? Ask the prison authorities, who with their Neanderthal reasoning have all the answers, but really have none that fit into dealing with the uncommon condition of transsexualism.

After six months when I finally arrived to live there full time on day parole it was such a relief. There were about eight of us who would be there for lengthy periods due to the length of our sentences. When I arrived there I still had a further ten years remaining to be served. The regulars among us became good friends. On weekdays I went morning and afternoon to life skills classes which consisted of everything from sewing to assertiveness training and, as at most halfway houses, drug therapy as well.

Once per week the place would be locked up and we would all head out to the YWCA for an hour or so. Missy, one of the residents, and I would usually do the weekly grocery shopping together. Missy had a big Chrysler with lots of room for groceries and with the two of us looking after the shopping, we always made sure we had what was needed and wanted. A female staff member would usually come along to pay the bill, but occasionally we would go on our own.

I managed to get some part-time work cleaning at the Hamilton Convention Centre a couple of nights per week and all in all things went very well. Don and I kept in touch by mail and phone and he sent me money to help with my weekly sessions of electrolysis. Don was earning good money while he was in Joyceville, having much responsibility and plenty of overtime. It felt good knowing he cared so much for me.

Don's sister Marg and I became good friends and would occasionally go to the movies, out for dinner or for walks in the woods. She gave me her sewing machine, which was only a few years old, when she received a new one for Christmas. I was doing repairs and alterations and making the odd item. When I finally left the halfway house someone had stolen it, along with many of my clothes and odds and ends.

When I was released to Elizabeth Fry in June, I made an appointment with the Gender Dysphoria Clinic at the Clarke Institute in Toronto, and the appointment date was set for approximately one year ahead. In May 1989 I had an interview with Clarke's gender team for the second time and I quote from their letter:

> *It is our opinion that you are transsexual and you should continue living in the female role.*

The Clarke Clinic required the transsexual person to work or go to school full time for two years prior to recommendation for surgery. However, due to the fact that I was on a disability pension I was not able to fill either of these requirements. I explained this to Dr. Steiner and also the fact that I had been fully functioning in my daily life as a woman for the past year.

Dr. Steiner agreed to take this into account, saying perhaps an exception could be made and asked to see me again in one year's time. This was quite depressing because up until now I had been assessed once by Vancouver specialists and twice by the Clarke gender team and all assessments were positive and in basic agreement. Then again there were the positive recommendations made by Dr. Laverty and his team at Kingston, Ontario.

I could hardly say I was pleased with the prospect of waiting yet another year and then it would be perhaps just another maybe. It was always like looking at a mirage in the desert; the closer I got the further away it seemed to move, but I had no choice except to remain patient and hope for the best. I continued living at the halfway house and everything continued to go fine. Don sent me money to buy and insure a car. I started helping a friend look after her sick parents. Her mother was bed-ridden and dying from cancer, so I would spend time at her bedside talking with her and helping with whatever was needed. Her father had a serious lung condition and problems with his legs and needed the aid of a walker to get around. We would go for daily walks of about an hour's duration. Linda, my friend, would clean house and prepare meals. Linda's children, aged 11 and 13, would hug me and call me "Aunt Kathy." This was very special to me. After about one year of electrolysis no one could tell that I was not an anatomical woman.

Then disaster struck again. Sylvie, a young woman from the house, took my car keys out of my jacket pocket without my knowledge or permission and took off in my car. She had quite a serious accident involving three other cars. When I arrived back at the house that afternoon a police officer was talking to the female staff member on duty.

The police officer asked if I had got into an accident with my car. Quite truthfully I answered no. The question was repeated several times until finally the officer said he was now past his shift time and wanted to get home. He told me that if I said it was me, he would simply write out tickets under the Highway Patrol Act and he'd be on his way. The alternative, he angrily offered, if I continued to deny it, was that he would handcuff me, lay criminal charges and take me into custody. I told him to go ahead and write the tickets as I was definitely not anxious for a return to prison.

Since Sylvie was much shorter than me, tan-skinned with short dark curly hair, I felt certain that the witnesses in court could not confuse her with me, given my height, slender build and fair colouring and hair. I received a summons to appear in court the next day and a trial date was set for several months ahead. After the police officer had left the house the female staff member on duty phoned Barb Hill, my parole officer, who in turn had the police come to the house that evening to arrest me and take me to the provincial jail lockup. They placed me in segregation, which was just as well.

The next day Barb came to see me and I told her I was not guilty, that I had only taken the tickets from the police officer to avoid going back to jail and also stressed to her that I would be found not guilty when the case came to court three months later.

I asked her if I could come back to the halfway house in the meantime and she refused. She thought I was guilty and told me so. I told her that if she were to see the Crown prosecutor in regard to four witness statements she would find that I was not guilty.

She refused so I remained in the city jail for three months. Needless to say I had the anger of the innocent and still find it difficult to understand why she did not do a little checking as I suggested, but to no avail. I was wasting my breath and energy in my efforts to get out. As they say, give a dog a bad name and he'll keep it.

Finally the trial date came up and I was found not guilty in about ten minutes of testimony from witnesses. Barb Hill's intransigence effectively sent me back to Joyceville for a period of time until I could get my parole reinstated.

I guess it was about September 1989 when I arrived back at Joyceville. At this time I estimated that I had about 27 months to serve and I would then be released with Don on mandatory supervision. No more halfway houses or hassles and we would be able to rent an apartment and live a life on our own and get away from the criminal element.

There was the incident in 1983 where I was totally innocent in a store robbery, but still I wound up with an extra three years and now this second incident with my car. Oh yes, I know there are lots of sceptics who on reading these protestations will scoff and assume that, being an ex-con, I cannot tell the truth. I decided after that not to allow myself to be put in similar situations in the future and therefore would serve my remaining 27 months inside. After all with all the time I had served, 27 months was a short time!

I asked to be put on the same range as Don, but at that point his range was full and no one wanted to change ranges. I was placed on range 4D, which consisted of mostly young fellows and they were sarcastic with all the usual expletives, making it known that I was not welcome as their neighbour.

The next day a guard called me to the office and was told that a senior official wanted to see me. This senior official in turn told me I was to be placed in segregation until they knew what to do with me.

Don went to the Prisoners' Committee and they managed to rearrange things, moving guys around and after a few days there were two cells on one range for Don and myself. We had some friends on this range also, so things were fine. During the fifteen months I had been out electrolysis had successfully removed such beard as I had and with a larger hormonal dosage my breasts had doubled in size.

In reality matters in prison had become worse for me due to this. I felt emotionally drained. I had been living with twelve other women for 15 months and had felt so good and peaceful. Then to be shipped back into a male institution was disturbing and awkward. There were sarcastic and lewd comments from some, roughness from others and sexual advances again as might be expected. The brutal Frenchman was still there and needless to say he caused me much anxiety. I applied for full parole "by exception" as I fitted one of three acceptable categories. The relevant words were "further incarceration was likely to cause emotional or physical damage."

This was not my first attempt to obtain parole by exception, but then as now, it was denied just like my attempts to gain transfer to a female prison. I was really caught like an animal in a trap. Forwards, backwards, sideways, up or down, nothing seemed to work to enable me to escape from the coils of the system and at least come into a scene more secure and amenable to my real emotional and security needs.

As I pointed out a little earlier there was something terribly contradictory. I could successfully live for 15 months in a women's halfway house but could not transfer to a women's prison. Don and I both wrote letters to Corrections Service Canada and to Federal Members of Parliament. The parliamentary people sided with me and I even had a lawyer from Kingston act in my behalf, but in the end I always lost. Fortunately, Don had become a part of my life. Without him I doubt if I would have survived in those final years. Many times I said, "Chain me into the sewer system with the rats. I'd be better off than living among these animals of men!"

There was a new doctor at Joyceville who quickly earned the nickname "the mechanic." He came to work with black grease under his nails and ingrained in the pores of his hands. He told me that his hobby was working on cars. This doctor liked me, though, and prescribed two Serax tranquilizers daily which would be equal to 10 mg of Valium. This helped a great deal with the constant anxiety I was feeling. He gave me pretty well what I asked for, stating correctly that I knew my body better than he did. This was a refreshing new approach!

Time went on and then it was Don's release date, but he didn't want to go, saying he would stay with me an extra ten months until my mandatory supervision date. There is no problem for a prisoner to sign off mandatory supervision for however long is requested.

About October 1991, my sister phoned me at Joyceville and wondered if I was coming back to Vancouver. First, I would contact Dr. Diane Watson at the Vancouver Gender Dysphoria Clinic and then call my sister back.

If I was to come back to Vancouver I asked, how long would it take me to get approval for surgery? Dr. Watson replied that if everything was the same as when she saw me in 1980 and I followed clinic instructions I could have approval within one year.

Don stated that he would stay with me forever, so I phoned my sister and told her my plans. On January 30th, 1992, I was released with Don on mandatory supervision. We travelled to Vancouver and what we hoped would be a new life for us both.

* * * * *

Don and I made our way to Vancouver by train. This trip was one of the happiest times in my life and we were met at the railway station by my loving sister who was so happy to see me. She accepted me as her sister, although she had only ever previously known me as her brother for the all-too-brief periods when I would show up between stints in prison.

Don and I stayed in motels for several days until we finally found an apartment in the upper east end of Vancouver. He would come with me to the Gender Dysphoria Clinic on a regular basis, and met and got on well with the psychiatrists and the psychologist. It was a new lease on life and we were very happy, particularly with the prospect of me having my long-awaited gender reassignment surgery, hopefully in the near future.

In February 1993 I was approved for surgery, but there was no funding available through the B.C. Medical Services Plan, even though it was available in other provinces. We were both very depressed by this development, but kept our disappointment under control as we continued to hope for greater progress towards adequate health insurance funding, as happened with other health conditions.

We conducted our lives in a very positive manner. Like millions of others we bought lottery tickets each week in the hope that a lucky windfall would provide the shortcut enabling me to have surgery.

Unfortunately, 18 months after our return to Vancouver, Don passed away at the age of 50. I was overwhelmed and felt very lost without him. He had been a source of enormous strength for me and knowing him as I did seemed to give me incentive for improvement in my life and the will to deal with ongoing problems.

After his death, being alone created new problems, but I continue hoping and praying, and surviving the best I can until the day I can make that great adjustment in my life. Like others, I had no choice in the way I was put together, but the will to survive is a powerful incentive. Sometimes when I think of my not-always-wanted escapes from death through suicide or prison homicide, I feel that the good Lord has preserved me through thick and thin, perhaps for something better one day.

* * * * *

PART TWO

by

Stephanie Castle

Prisoner of Gender

Chapter Eight

Transsexualism Described

Transsexuals, above all, seek the internal harmony that comes to them from identifying themselves as proper and accepted members of the opposite sex. The wearing of the clothes of that sex has no separate importance for them, save as it may be symbolically relevant once the sex reassignment is achieved. They are not content to fulfil their sexual fantasies in homosexual activity. Despite recent legal changes in many jurisdictions, such activity remains socially stigmatized and religiously forbidden. In many places it is also legally outlawed. Recent Queensland legislation referring to "deviates" and "perverts" shows that, in some quarters, these attitudes to homosexuality and homosexual conduct are not a thing of the past. Transsexuals want none of this. They seek integration into society and the peace that comes from social acceptance. They seek to earn this acceptance, bearing the talisman of radical surgical intervention designed to bring their external sexual organs into harmony with their minds.

This description is taken from *Sex Change: Medical and Legal Aspects of Sex Reassignment* (Tasmania, 1988) by H.A. Finlay, a Barrister at Law and at the time of publication,

Associate Professor of Law at Monash University, Melbourne, and Dr. Wm. A.W. Walters, Professor of Reproductive Medicine at the University of Newcastle, N.S.W., Australia. As leading experts in the fields of transsexual law and medicine they drew on Justice M.D. Kirby, President of the Court of Appeal, Supreme Court of New South Wales for a foreword to their book. Justice Kirby contributed the above quoted wisdom.

Dr. Gerald Ramsey in his book *Transsexuals: Candid Answers to Private Questions* (Freedom, Cal., 1996) expressed it very well when he wrote:

> *The transsexual process is not a flight of fancy. It is the persistant pursuit of physical, emotional, social, spiritual and sexual wholeness, accomplished at enormous personal cost.*

* * * * *

The existence of the Female-to-Male transsexual condition is recognized, but the essentials of almost everything in this chapter deal with the Male-to-Female condition except where specified.

Throughout this text the words *transsexualism* and *gender dysphoria* will recur. Many readers will be unfamiliar with either, particularly the second, so at this point it is desirable to develop a definition of each. While they are used interchangeably there is a small technical difference in their meaning.

Transsexualism is a word which came into public use around the end of the 1940s or early 1950s. While the late Dr. Harry Benjamin, the New York endocrinologist, did not invent it, it could certainly be claimed that he popularized the term. Benjamin, it should be added, was one of the early great pioneers in transsexual medicine. When his book *The Transsexual Phenomenon* came out in 1966, the word had become a matter of common usage as by then a number of well-publicized so-called sex changes had made the news.

Transsexualism is the condition and the process by which a person seeks to take on the **physical** *characteristics of the opposite sex.* The emphasis is on the word *physical* as to a large extent the mental characteristics are already there and have been present from the first moment of self-recognition in the affected person. Under the influence of hormone therapy and psychiatric counselling the physical characteristics will come into line with the mental characteristics, and following surgery the process becomes accomplished. Because of the absence of the original natural source of hormones and the continuing application of the hormones of the new adopted sex, the mental and physical states lock in together and a new harmonious whole results.

This, of course, is in contrast to the situation prior to treatment, when the physical and mental states are out of harmony with each other. This is *gender dysphoria* which may then be described as the *symptom of transsexualism*. It is this disharmony or incongruency which creates such discomfort or even mental agony at times in the sufferer. It can influence his or her mind, sometimes quite irrationally.

The condition is always long-term. If its origins are taken into account in every sense it is a lifetime condition. Most commonly it manifests itself between earliest infancy and pre-pubescence. It is a natural although abnormal condition which further develops concurrent with the growth in the physical and intellectual capacity of the subject. It is not an indication of sexual orientation. It cannot be dismissed as hallucinatory or some sort of mental disease.

No one catches it, no one can transmit it, it does not develop because of reading or seeing something. One does not learn to be a transsexual, as it is there prior to birth, its origin being the result of a prenatal biological malfunction by which the brain as a result maladjusts itself in terms of the underlying biological sex. The popular press and much of the public think of it as a sex change, perhaps in itself a more exciting concept than anything less than that. In truth, such a thing is only partly achievable—and then some would call it cosmetic. What it is is a gender change with gender defined by one's assessment of oneself. The mental state tells a male person that he is in fact female even though this is contradicted by the physical reality. This is termed *gender dysphoria*. What gender reassignment surgery does is create the situation by which a reasonable facsimile of female organs are created or develop, but the process cannot be complete in every sense as it is impossible to replicate the female reproductive organs. Gender reassignment surgery helps complete the gender identity and is actually much more than so-called sex change. It usually settles the identity crisis which might actually be a bigger overall issue than the actual surgery involved.

The theory of the actual process in nature is not exact, because whenever the condition is discovered it has long since gone through its formative stage. What is believed to happen is that the hormone balance in the foetus is disturbed at a critical time in the foetal development. This may occur around the tenth week of pregnancy when the male and female aspects of the brain are starting to develop by the process known as brain differentiation. This process anchors the normal intellectual, sensory and emotional attributes of the brains of the two sexes. There are differences between the male and female brain which when fully developed portray the differing mental features and emotional characteristics of the two sexes: the male and female personalities.

This happens despite the influence of the chromosomal sex, by which XX chromosomes indicate a girl while XY indicate a boy. At this point let us add that chromosomal sex is of itself not an infallible indicator as was once thought. There are women with only the first functioning X which usually results in an ultra feminine person. There are women, sometimes with masculine features and an interest in sport, with XY chromosomes who would have been men had the Y been fully functional, and to be a male the Y has to be fully functional.

It is possible that the process actually predates brain differentiation to the point when it may be established that a faulty gene, like so many other genetically based diseases and conditions, is at the centre of the establishment of this condition. This may rank as pure supposition at this stage, but scientific study is constantly pushing back the frontiers of genetic medicine, so it seems quite possible that future research will open new avenues assisting understanding of this complex condition.

English author Liz Hodgkinson in her book *Bodyshock: The Truth about Changing Sex* (London, 1987) quotes from an article dating back to 1980 that appeared in the British Journal of Sexual Medicine. This article advanced the theory that a substance called the H-Y antigen has a role in the proper establishment of the brain's sexual function. According to this theory the H-Y antigen functions as the "glue" in adequately fixing testosterone's role as the sex hormone in XY chromosome foetuses. If this glue is not present in sufficient quantity then the testosterone does not "take" in sufficient strength and thus a sexual abnormality might develop prior to birth. This may also explain the statement made above about women with XY chromosomes, in that the lack of the H-Y antigen might have allowed the Y chromosome to become inadequate or nonfunctional.

When gender dysphoria shows up at an early age it is usually termed a primary dysphoria. When gender dysphoria shows up in later life often coupled with an incident kicking off great stress and anxiety, it is usually referred to as a secondary dysphoria. It does seem that in a great many cases both primary and secondary dysphorias are present.

The hormones do have a critical role in the development of the foetus prior to the point when brain differentiation begins. It is the presence in adequate quantities of the male sex hormone, testosterone, or the female sex hormone, estrogen, that triggers the development of the gonads, and from that, brain differentiation develops. It is the chromosome blueprint which starts up the motors so that the XY generates the initial presence of testosterone and the XX likewise with estrogen.

The hormone flow can be disturbed in a variety of ways, some natural and others unnatural. One thing appears certain, and that is that the male foetus undergoes a drenching of testosterone at about the thirteenth week of pregnancy, while no equivalent drenching of estrogen occurs in the female foetus. Precisely what throws the female foetus off to eventually become a female-to-male transsexual is not suggested here unless a renegade testosterone in some way occurs. The drenching of the male foetus appears to be rather like "fixing" film in the photographic development process. Such a drenching also occurs at male puberty, causing the voice to break, muscle, beard and body hair development, and accelerating masculine sexual responses.

Disturbance in the hormonal flow might occur because of emotional upset in the mother, injury during pregnancy, or the application of medications during pregnancies—in short anything which disturbs the natural balance.

As noted, transsexualism is not confined to men alone. Far from it. Such statistics as are available suggest that the incidence of the condition in women, while not as widespread, may represent between 30 and 40 per cent of all cases. That would be in line with the experience at Vancouver Hospital's Gender Dysphoria Clinic in British Columbia, but Walters and Ross in *Transsexualism and Sex Reassignment* (Melbourne, 1985) mention a Czech estimate of as high as 50 per cent of all cases in that country are in the female-to-male category. Ramsey in *Transsexuals: Candid Questions to Private Questions* notes that disparities in figures probably indicate that in smaller more centrally controlled European countries figures may be more reliable because of the greater ease of assembling national statistics. In a country such as Canada, with four established clinics and individual specialist consultants spread across the country, there appears to be little exchange of data between the points where information might be expected to accumulate.

A notable feature about many transsexuals is that even if their memory on other matters is hazy, the circumstances of their first self-discovery of their gender dysphoria is branded into their memory in incredibly sharp detail. My own self-discovery goes back to the age of three and I remember it today as though it happened only yesterday. It certainly occurred long before there was any appreciation of human sexuality and this is not at all uncommon. My co-author shared the same experience, her memory being clear that the first recollection occurred while she was still a pre-schooler.

Most transsexuals will confirm that the first discovery was euphoric, a pleasant escape from day-to-day reality. It is mysterious as one cannot relate it at first to anything else in one's life. As one becomes older it not only takes on the form of a fantasy, but can also be erotic to some extent. My experience was that erotic aspects really related to pleasurable contentment rather than anything wildly stimulating. It became my secret to contemplate and fantasize over, particularly at times of anxiety or extreme loneliness. The fantasy, which might almost take on the form of a second separate personality, is not disturbing in any destructive sense, but has palliative qualities hiding the subject from unpleasant realities. This seems to be a frequent pattern in others.

Transsexualism is invariably confused with homosexuality. However, the two are quite distinct as will be explained a little later. What usually becomes apparent to most is that societal stereotypes tend to condemn anything sexual which is different. Often there is little if any understanding of the condition by those in a subject's family or social group who may be close to the subject. Most commonly if anything should ever leak out then it becomes something to deny, to shut out and sometimes even treat as a disgusting aberration. Judgements are made and invariably settle on sexual issues. There is little if any understanding that the subject has been carrying all sorts of loose mental baggage around for an entire lifetime. This can waste enormous stretches of the most productive periods of the subject's life in unsettled anxiety, stress and fretting over something to which there seems no reasonable answer and little hope of a solution. It is small wonder that many transsexuals come to clinics for treatment to be confronted first with the need to deal positively with a substance dependency like drugs and alcohol. In their past this has been their only unsatisfactory answer to dealing with the personal pressures of gender dysphoria.

As we are all sexual creatures and life itself spins on our sexual heritage and respective roles there should be little surprise that this of all segments of the human mosaic is far and away the most tantalizing and fascinating. For many, when things go wrong sexually it can represent the most horrible manifestations of the dark side of human existence. But to judge transsexualism as a wholly sexual issue is way off the mark. Yes, transsexuals do have sexual instincts like everyone else, but dealing with it is dealing with an issue of mental health first and foremost. I did not go through gender change to satisfy carnal urges as they applied to either sex. I dealt with it as a pressing issue for the sake of my own survival, and if it had not been dealt with I doubt that I would be sitting here today writing these words. More likely my ashes would by now have been consigned to the sea.

At school the transsexual is likely to have a hard time if he or she makes any admission to such a condition within, and if there is pronounced evidence of effeminacy or a gender change, then it will attract increasing attention according to the scale of events. If the subject belongs to, or is exposed to extreme beliefs such as a fundamentalist religious denomination, he can expect to be offered hellfire and damnation if he is unable or unwilling to subjugate himself wholly to that denomination's ideas. Fundamentalist religious thinking frequently characterizes transsexualism as being the work of the devil. Typically the fundamentalists claim that the condition can be cured if the sufferer will "give himself to the Lord."

Fear of all these forces or influences usually causes the subject to self-repress. Self-repression means that one's mental processes become choked with worries and anxieties, while emotional responses are so distorted that they cannot give a true representation of the inner person. Anxiety can be so severe that one anxiety feeds on another in a mounting spiral of uncertainty and crisis. At such times a complete functional breakdown may occur, meaning a total loss of confidence, loss of self-esteem and development of a sense of worthlessness. Alternatively, a subject may embark on senseless irrational acts which seem to be a needed safety valve to let off pressure.

Such repression can be one of the most painful influences in the life of a transsexual, possibly more agonizing than any other single influence. One of the great reliefs is the day, after much agonizing in secret, when one finally decides to unburden oneself of these worries to a sympathetic person, maybe a doctor or social worker or just an understanding relative or friend. For many, learning to talk about one's own problem may be like learning to walk again. For others it is like releasing a flood gate bathed in tears. Once it all flows forth, the greatest difficulty then becomes knowing when to stop. Not that it's ever easy, and even on occasion one might miscalculate and find the person in whom you have decided to confide is less than sympathetic which might be very disconcerting.

There are two situations which cause much confusion. One is that people commonly assume that a transvestite is the same as a transsexual. Even though the condition of transvestitism is classified as a milder form of dysphoria (see Watson Table, Group 1 and 2, Appendix I), the relationship between the two is somewhat tenuous. Transvestitism is thought to be largely confined to heterosexual men, but some commentators have made the suggestion recently that there is such a thing as female transvestitism and this author is inclined to agree. In fact, a much-respected female friend admits to enjoying wearing mostly male clothes and not just facsimiles of same. What is she if she is not a transvestite? Transvestites are often thrill dressers, i.e. they do it for the excitement, for a sexual high and they have no interest in any permanent change. In fact, they are often out of sympathy with transsexuals, whom they may well regard as being mentally unstable or worse. The transsexual, on the other hand, often views the transvestite as being a shallow exhibitionist only interested in surface effect and with no appreciation of the gender core issue[2] faced by the

---

[2] While transvestism is only of peripheral interest in this book, an excellent and sensitive account of a relationship with a transvestite is given by Monica Jay in *Geraldine: For the Love of a Transvestite*, London 1985.

transsexual. It should be noted that some transvestites do cross-dress solely as a means of relaxation.

Gay transvestites are often *drag queens* or *she-males* and occupy a particular place in the homosexual world. Drag queens tend to be overdone or larger-than-life. Often they present a parody of what a natural woman actually is. Some are highly talented and are to be found in theatrical roles in nightclubs and bars which cater to the type of life they relate to. There is usually little to be found in common with true transsexuals, who invariably seek a normal life as a woman devoid of the elements of showmanship or exhibitionism associated with the drag queens.

There is a midway category called the *transvestitic-transsexual*. They are not driven by motives associated with sexual gratification, but do become transsexual over time (Watson Table, Group 3, Appendix I). It is more than likely that the original spark which causes transsexualism is actually present even though it does not become apparent until adulthood. Such people would likely be categorized as having a secondary gender dysphoria.

The other situation concerns *homosexuality.* It is often assumed that transvestites and transsexuals are gay and that the three conditions are one and the same. This is totally wrong. Homosexuality, like its counterpart heterosexuality, is a sexual orientation. A homosexual can be and usually is normal in every way except for his sexual preference favouring his or her own sex, whereas most transvestites and transsexuals come from a heterosexual background by which their sexual orientation favours the opposite sex.

With heterosexual transsexuals it does not always follow that they will swing over to a preference for the new opposite sex. In fact it is more likely that a significant number will retain the old preference for their original opposite sex and some may become bisexual. However, there is some fluidity here as it might take a gender reassigned person some time to settle his or her exact sexual preferences. In homosexual transsexuals it sometimes follows that their preference is for heterosexual men, a combination which is almost certain to be unattainable until after surgery, when they can then become heterosexual women and therefore, in theory, enter into a regular relationship with a heterosexual man.

It should be added that the empirical evidence today is more than ever supporting the idea that homosexuality also starts in the pre-birth period in a way similar to the start of transsexualism, although it affects different aspects of the brain including the hypothalamus, a section of the brain which governs responses of the sympathetic nervous system such as body temperature. In homosexual men in some instances the hypothalamus has been found to have smaller sub-structures. Researchers have noted that this combination is about equivalent to that of a biological woman.

While dealing with the hypothalamus, a very recent report released by the Netherlands Institute for Brain Research in Amsterdam[3] reported preliminary evidence that transsexuals may be inherently different. Their study covered six male-to-female transsexuals and took place over a period of 11 years until each volunteer had died. It showed that a tiny structure deep within a part of the brain controlling sexual function appeared to be more like that found in women rather than men. This was discerned after a comparison with the brains of two dozen ordinary men and women. The difference noted concerned a group of neurons called the BSTc. In both heterosexual and homosexual men this

---

[3] Noted from a report in *Time* magazine, November 3, 1995, entitled *Trapped in the Body of a Man* by Christine Gorman. A similar report was also carried in some scientific journals including *New Scientist* and *Nature*.

has been noted to be 50 per cent bigger than in women. In the case of the transsexuals' brains the BSTc was in marked contrast to that of normal men. It was much closer to that of the female brain in terms of size. This study is interesting as it tends to confirm that the beliefs held by many transsexuals about themselves are not mere figments of an overactive imagination. More and more research is pointing to the probability that these beliefs do have a basis in fact.

Just briefly, there is one final human condition which it would be appropriate to mention, if only to dispel doubts that some people have when the subject comes up. This concerns *fetishisms*, a group of conditions which really relate to the outer fringes of sex. The most usual form arises when a material, garment or other inanimate object is used as an aid to bring about sexual arousal. Festishes may range from harmless minor responses to a full play act involving dressing in elaborate fetishist clothes of leather, vinyl or rubber. Sometimes these rituals are associated with bondage and masochism. Occasionally transvestitism can have fetishistic overtones, but in no sense do fetishes have any relationship to transsexualism. For many otherwise normal people fetishes are distinct turn-ons which are pursued often with great objectivity.

* * * * *

Regardless of the point in the text, we shall refer to Katherine or Douglas in the feminine gender as Kathy from here on except when quoting from official documents or relaying actual dialogue if appropriate.

Kathy Johnson became a severely aggrieved child following her mother's untimely death when Kathy was three and a half years old, as noted a common age for self-discovery of something different within, which gives the first indication of recognizable transsexualism. The death of her mother would be a disaster for any child, but in this case Kathy and her sister had all their roots disturbed. Obviously their father could not look after them on a daily basis as he had to earn a living to support them all, but apart from that there did not appear to have been much bonding between father and children on account of his indifference and the macho belief that bringing up children was a woman's role alone. The process of shunting them around, which has already been detailed, was bad enough, but the knowledge that they were deprived of their mother even if they did not fully understand the nature of death, must have been profoundly disturbing to them.

Kathy was clearly highly strung, but the loss of her mother, the coming into her life of a brutal new stepmother, and the failure of the father to provide any counterbalance to the stepmother must have further aggravated the child's hyper-sensitivity. As noted, transsexuals are deeply sensitive which might have accounted for the greater difficulty Kathy had in accommodating to the negative influence of the stepmother.

Rebellious resistance to the stepmother seems to have been Kathy's main response until she went to school. Being constantly on her guard against the stepmother probably started or aggravated the development of an antisocial attitude so that when she went to school, which usually has a broadening effect on young children, she found herself feeling uncomfortable, particularly in the company of boys. Her antisocial attitude and the stresses it caused within probably had a negative effect on her learning ability, but the fact that she was able to rise above this and catch up on her education when in institutions indicates that the inability to assimilate was not a permanent affliction. It was clearly caused by the adverse environmental influences already recounted. Today she is an intelligent sensitive woman, well-read, well-spoken and she has writing potential. So who and what failed?

The first breakdown was parental. The circumstances were tragic for reasons already described. The stepmother lodged into the fabric of family life like an unwelcome tumor. She effectively blocked communication with the children's father who displayed considerable weakness in the face of a dominant spouse, even though today Kathy talks of her father as being a good man. Despite Kathy's kindly mention of her father, it is of interest to note that he built the family home during the lifetime of Kathy's mother. It was no doubt her dream home in which to raise her family. When the father died every possession he had, including the house, went to the domineering second wife, both children being left the princely sum of one dollar!

The stepmother probably also had the same negative effect in terms of the all-important communication between school and parents. Obviously deeply disturbed, Kathy really needed professional help at the outset of her difficulties and while the first impulse would be to blame the authorities alone, a school has little chance of getting through to unresponsive parents. This does not release the school from responsibility, as there are, after all, other agencies to which they can turn, but in those days in the 1950s the answer was more punitive, with less thought being given to specialized counselling. Today, counselling would have been given a higher priority, but unless a child is in really deep trouble the process is still very slow in responding unless the matter can be handled at school counsellor level, or privately through a consultant.

Today also certain specialists in nutrition might have tested Kathy for dietary deficiencies. We all need a proper balance of critical vitamins and trace elements in our diet. For example a recent report, presented at the annual meeting of the Society of Neuroscience, states that William Walsh and colleagues at the Health Research Centre in Skokie, Ill., found elevated copper-zinc ratios in violent boys. I am not suggesting that Kathy suffered from this imbalance as she was certainly not a violent offender, but considering how she lived when young by stealing food, which at least for convenience was always packaged or processed, she might well have stuffed herself with sugars or other ingredients known to be harmful if consumed to excess. These might have activated what ultimately would be described as hyperglycemia or even hypoglycemia, and that in turn would have increased her anxieties and antisocial behaviour. I know it can exist as at one time a member of my own family suffered in precisely this manner as a result of sugar addiction.

There is no evidence that Kathy had any form of psychological counselling until she ended up at Brannan Lake school at age 11. Instead matters went from bad to worse in the local school system, until the school authorities felt they could handle her no longer. As she herself recalled she was mostly living on the street, starting the process of petty pilferage for food by which she largely lived. She was no longer welcome in her own home so resorted to sleeping secretively in the crawl space under the family home, effectively abandoned by her own family. One has to wonder where the social agencies were during this time, although it has to be ackowledged also that street-wise kids know well enough how to avoid the authority represented by the social workers.

Even in spite of tensions between parents and offspring, few parents would be unconcerned about the whereabouts of their child. This did not seem to happen in Kathy's case, although it is remarkable that she had such strong, if misplaced, homing instincts when one recalls her habit of sleeping in the crawl space under the house.

* * * * *

Earlier Kathy makes reference to her first encounter with a Vancouver pyschiatrist with a reputation for understanding transsexualism. She obviously visited this practitioner hoping for more help and certainly expecting a good deal more than she received. She was to be disappointed. While a medical specialist is consulted to form an opinion, and may indeed believe that the opinion so expressed was as much as he could present taking into account the nature of his referral from the prison doctor, was this really good enough?

Of course it wasn't. It was, in fact, a hopeless diagnosis if one could dignify it as being a diagnosis, but it was typical of almost her entire experience while in prison—too little, too late. In 1967 quite a lot was known about transsexualism on an international basis. Research papers and authoritative books were already available to which any so-called expert would have had access, although it has to be stated in fairness that a veritable flood of written material was published after Kathy had her interview.

There will be a number of references to prison doctors and specialists throughout the text which follows. The reports of outside recognised gender dysphoria specialist consultants all agreed in Kathy's favour. The remainder composed of medical professionals within the prison structure were almost universally callous, indifferent and betrayed a notable lack of genuine knowledge. These ignorant reports included those of senior prison officials only too ready to accept the reports of prison doctors and non-gender experts as coming "as if from the Lord on high." The enlightened gender experts were not the ones who appeared to decide in the decision-making process. It was too often a case of the blind leading the blind.

Kathy's problems were also compounded by the times in which she was going through her worst crises. There was no gender dysphoria clinic in Vancouver until 1985, and little in the way of formal organization of any sort in Canada other than the Clarke Institute of Psychiatry, a guru-like institution in Toronto. The people who run the Vancouver Clinic today were younger and less experienced in that period. Their credibility was not as fully established as it is today. Sexism was rampant, so how could female specialists be believed by men in matters like these?

There is evidence that the attitude of medical practitioners is also changing with the times. When I was a youngster, a doctor along with a lawyer, a senior parish priest and a few other professionals were considered next to God and many of them acted as if they knew it. There was at one time an attitude that one should not question the doctor as he knew best. Doctors of the old school did not feel that they were under any obligation to discuss the details of a potentially fatal illness within a family as it was not good for the patient, and a soon-to-be widow might grieve prematurely.

Today a modern view calls for a more open relationship between a doctor and the patient. This even leads to an atmosphere in some instances where the pursuit of treatment will more likely be a joint venture between doctor and patient. Personally, I like that approach. It acknowledges that I am an intelligent human being capable of thinking for myself. In fact, one doctor friend said to me, "I listen to the patient; very often she's right."

If indeed gross negligence is a factor here, then it goes right to the top in the prison management structure. I lack the legal education to form a solid assessment, but as a lay person I believe that there are grounds for action. I know this as a taxpayer and a business person with considerable business savvy and experience. As well, I am a citizen who is forever being asked to further shoulder the burden of years of government mismanagement. In Kathy's case, if nothing else, there was severe mismanagement and the cost to the taxpayer in the end was enormous.

A course of treatment would have reduced this cost by a lesser but still considerable amount. In February 1995, Canadian Press in a news report quoted prison authorities as stating that it costs $70,000 a year to keep a prisoner in maximum security and $36,000 for minimum security. The figures are staggering. How the costs were arrived at was not stated, but presumably everything from prison staff salaries to amortization of buildings and installations was factored in. Equivalent U.S. figures recently released through the American media are quite a lot lower so without establishing exact parameters comparisons might be misleading.

A wrongdoer is required to pay society for her crimes. Kathy knew that then and acknowledges it now. But when the system takes custody of that self-same human being, the system on behalf of society is charged with her well-being and safe return to society suitably rehabilitated; at least that is the situation in theory and the supposed aim of the system. It has no authority to allow the infliction of torture or judge that because she is a time-serving convict she is beyond the pale in terms of proper medical treatment and safekeeping. It is no excuse to claim in defence that she was only treated like all others and this may be so, but to place a sacrificial goat, given her obvious femininity and the natural instincts which came with it, into the lion's den was about the way it was handled. Anyone with a modicum of compassion and common sense could have seen that there was something intrinsically wrong with Kathy, who typically of a transsexual, and in spite of every conceivable threat, insisted against all odds that she was a woman. In true transsexuals this insistence and the burning desire coupled with it are the twin features which are usually unchangeable.

Was her act the behaviour of an insane person? No, it was the act of an extreme sufferer from gender dysphoria, and we have seen already and shall see again later, to what desperate extremes she had to go in order to gain the attention of the system.

There is no suggestion here that gender reassignment surgery should be provided on demand. It has no parallel with going to the dentist and asking for a tooth to be pulled. Having been through the complete process, I am fully aware of the need for assessment in depth. No one needs mistakes in diagnosis, least of all the patient. No psychiatrist can make up his or her mind on one interview alone and second opinions can always be obtained and are a standard part of a clinical routine. There are never more than a handful of transsexuals enmeshed in the prison system. The example of Jill, described by Kathy in her narrative, exemplifies how rank stupidity far outweighs ordinary considerations of common humanity in the operation of the prison system. One wonders why it should be such an unassailable problem to see them properly concentrated together in one or two institutions where they would be able to receive appropriate supervision and treatment without the daily hell of terror, harassment, brutalization and the sexual assault they are otherwise exposed to.

* * * * *

At the commencement of this chapter we quoted two excerpts from the works of Australian and American authors, both of whom, we felt, caught the spirit and nature of transsexualism more perfectly and with more humanity than any words we have found elsewhere. The reader is invited to read them again as a closing to this chapter before moving on.

* * * * *

Chapter Nine

Sisyphus, the King of Corinth

A very sad, very tragic young man. A host of problems essentially related to his sexual identity.

So go the opening words of a meeting of parole board members to consider the case of Douglas M. Johnson, No. 69463A, some ten years later on in our narrative. Unfortunately, in 1970 Kathy was fully ten years away from even having these words spoken in her behalf, ten years of tragic events of nightmarish proportions while the hell continued.

Just why should the reader believe that there are actually human beings who suffer so deeply and are hurt so badly by events and actions beyond their control? Most of us might be tempted to regard it all as purest fiction, or if not fiction then some manifestation of insanity.

Why would any man want to do the things he has to do in order to be a woman? They are that lesser half of the human species, so essential to the continuation of mankind and yet so often downtrodden and denigrated that today women in many parts of the world often are seen as, and in fact are, a disenfranchised majority. To be sure in our society they have the vote, property rights and are not totally dependent on forming a union with a man as a means to survival. They endure incredible hardships often as single women to maintain a home life for their children, and suffer a far higher proportion of sexual, physical and psychological abuse from the men in their lives, than the men themselves do.

In modern society they increasingly have control of their own bodies and this is now a central feature in any United Nations considerations of the challenges of overpopulation. But in truth the ways in which they are put down are often far more subtle, and once a transsexual person has crossed the great divide between the sexes and becomes a woman, that is something he/she is likely to learn from experience.

I was once asked this question of "why?" and it is a difficult question to answer in everyday terms. It takes a little time to answer also, even if one understands the intricate nature of it all. In fact, seeking to give explanations rather than create justification was the thrust throughout my book *Feelings: A Transsexual's Explanation of a Baffling Condition.* Explanation can be supported by facts and case histories. Justification can become a quicksand of misunderstanding and while there are considerable elements of this in Kathy's story the intent is always to seek well-qualified explanation to back up the need for justification.

But why? That is a lot like saying why are your eyes brown and mine blue? More to the point, why am I gender dysphoric and my two younger brothers evidently unaffected? Why is it found in one member of an entire generation in a family group and may even be the first known case in an entire family history? We shall never know the history of previous generations in this regard, as there was no understanding of the condition of transsexualism, even though there are references to people in Greek mythology who might have been transsexual if their circumstances could be brought up to the understanding of the subject in modern times.

The answer to "why?" has already been given in technical terms as it relates to our biology and pre-natal formation and while the main circumstances of transsexualism from one person to another have mostly common features, the details of our individual lives can vary very widely.

To illustrate the helplessness of the transsexual caught in the prison system and to refute the frequently expressed public perception that prisoners in many ways have a cushy time of things, I have to delve deeply into personal examples to make my points in comparing the relative positions of the imprisoned and the free citizen.

In my own case which I regard as an example of total repression, I discovered my early symptoms at age three, but I never told a living soul. By the time I was nineteen I had identified my symptoms correctly as it turned out, even though the word "transsexualism" had not even been invented. This was as a result of reading Nils Hoyer's book *Man Into Woman*, an historic account of the first known gender reassignment operation, and that reading was back in the mid-1940s. I want to repeat an earlier point: Hoyer's book did not create the circumstances of my transsexualism. I caught nothing infectious from it, but it did help me more clearly define a personal problem I had been aware of since earliest remembered childhood.

I quickly learned to dismiss it from my mind, or at least so I thought, but it would come back like a phantom sent to haunt me. My characteristics include great determination and a mind that tends to plan things in depth like a well-conceived military manoeuvre. When I have followed through with my planning in depth in this manner things in this life have generally worked well for me. When I have become careless it has always been in conjunction with abandoning my usual strategies and then things have not gone so well and have even become the source of anxiety and grinding worry. I am not sure whether the carelessness has always preceded the anxiety, or the anxiety has been the source of becoming careless.

In any event when the anxiety took over I would find that my retreat into my inner fantasy world would be where I could find comfort. My mind would somehow seem to separate from my body and leave my physical presence staring into space in something of a trance-like way. The voice of my spouse, perhaps not liking to feel that she was shut out of my thoughts, might then shatter the entire illusion by asking what I was thinking about. My mind would have to then go into reverse gear as I thought of something plausible for an answer.

Such an answer might be, "Oh, I am thinking about the bills I have to pay tomorrow and where the money is coming from." I could never own up to the truth of what was on my mind. If I had done so, it might have been best in a strong relationship, but I feared the consequences. Neither of my two marriages had sat on unshakeable foundations and the last thing I was looking for was a marital break-up. When I did finally reveal the truth towards the end of my second marriage it was a bad experience which only served to hasten the end of a very shaky relationship.

When I did go into what I term "my greatest crisis" I suffered a great deal of mental pain. The reason for this situation was extreme religious pressure, my defence against which was to sink into a state of melancholia and from there I overate and overdrank. From being a very self-confident, highly objective person I was reduced for short periods to a blubbering wreck. My eyes would fill with tears, my nostrils would burn, I would have to find somewhere to hide so that I could have a quiet weep usually because I felt terribly sorry for myself. I lost my confidence, I developed an inferiority complex and lost my sense of self-esteem. How had I fallen into this trap? The highly objective me gave way to a timid self who could only think in terms of how to get from one meal to the next, or through one day at a time. At times I was suicidal, although, unlike Kathy, I never did translate my thoughts into action.

The importance in having treatment from someone who understood and could interpret my ambivalence was never more important than the day I walked into the clinic for the first time. I was near breaking point, but as usual with my "stiff upper lip" I was determined not to cave in. I had no idea what to expect and was actually feeling quite defensive and conspicuous as if the world was eavesdropping on my thoughts, even though there were only two or three Clinic staff visible. But in a way which at the time seemed uncanny, the two psychiatrists who interviewed me together seemed to know what they were talking about. They talked in terms I could relate to. They might have even anticipated some of my answers on the basis that I was telling them of a typical history.

When my appointment was over I felt much better. This was the occasion when I first unburdened myself of the first stages of a lifelong secret to someone who seemed to understand and it felt as though I had already removed a very heavy weight from my shoulders. At least two more interviews followed and with each my confidence returned fairly quickly. My objectivity came back and took on new forms. My self-esteem was elevated and I started to enjoy some success in a life which had been foundering.

The greatest satisfaction of all came at that point, because I had been able to cast off the shroud of obstinate secrecy which had inhibited most of my life. My two personalities were starting to merge. The masculine self would in my case never entirely disappear as happens with some transsexuals, but the female self would come into the ascendency and it became a happy union with which I am able to live in comfort and security.

Now, the reader may think that if this constituted a cure, like getting over a fever of some sort, why not put it all out of the mind and carry on with life as it was before, but as a person with reborn confidence. Fine, that would be the answer if I was not gender dysphoric in the first case. But in my case I was gender dysphoric and my newly reborn confidence came about simply because I had been honest with myself as a first step, and then followed honesty with others and an enormous relief at shedding my secret, even though getting it out at first was something like drawing the teeth of a tiger. Once the demon was released it just kept flooding out in a feeling of enormous relief. To this day I can talk and write about my experiences with complete confidence, unlike a few short years ago.

Nothing now on this good earth would persuade me to retreat back to the way I used to be, and nothing would persuade me that what I did for myself was not the right course of action for me.

I know, having gone the entire route, that I am a happier, more creative person. I have regained my drive but now it goes in directions more in keeping with my view of, and relationships with, other people. I have lost my aggressive, self-centred, all-pervading ambition to make lots of money, to be a big wheel, to shake things up. At the end of the day it is more important for me to think with satisfaction of what I did for someone less fortunate than myself, than to count the shekels which perhaps represent my monetary success. So long as I have my health, a comfortable apartment, my small business and my car, those are for the most part reward enough. However, I have the bonus of a strong relationship with my children, relatives and key friends who survived what for them must have been something of a crisis, as it was for me. Over and above that I have the reward of many wonderful friends, some old who have stood by me with much loyalty and understanding, and some new, and all in their way have enriched my life.

Yes, now that I am a woman, legally, functionally and philosophically, I live as a woman. I wear female clothes and make-up. I like to feel appropriately dressed for an occasion, but I do my best to wear sensible work clothes when I am going about my business and am not enslaved to any false images. I give little conscious thought to either except when checking myself before a mirror. I am not looking for a man, being quite happy with myself, my own company and with the tasks I set for myself and the recreational activities I enjoy. The fact that I am like I am at this point in my life is very natural. It would be strange for example if I now tried to ape a man. Nor do I see myself as in any way being a crossdresser. That is for the transvestites and that is something I have never been, no matter what went on in my mind.

What I have described is the essence of being a transsexual, a gender dysphoric, a gender conflicted person or call it what you will. Until you have confronted and fully dealt with your need to fully change the direction of your life there can be no real peace. There is constant frustration. One wastes an enormous amount of lifetime energy in fretting, sweating and agonizing in much the same way as Sisyphus, the King of Corinth in Greek mythology, who for his earthly misdeeds was condemned by the Gods to forever be rolling a large stone uphill only to have it roll down again just before reaching the top. It seems like an enormous hill ahead carrying a very heavy burden for a person like Kathy, still confronting the need to bring her body into line with her mind, but once that hill is finally climbed and that burden laid down, life takes on new meaning in terms of peace, relaxation and all the other good things which for the person in transit sometimes seems like a mirage.

* * * * *

Several days ago I had dinner with a friend who is going through gender change right now. She was a big aggressive man, a success story in the media, a person who told her mother at age 15 all about her gender dysphoria "problem." When she married she told her new wife of her crossdressing and the fact that she should have been born a woman, so that there could never be any laying of a charge of marrying under false pretences.

But this was not enough to ensure a happy life. There was something missing which seemed unattainable. Alcohol and drugs seemed to provide some relief from recurring nagging worries and anxieties and as time went on they took over her life. She made a good living in her field so that the supply of what she needed to feed her addictions was easily obtained. She would have been defined as an urban middle-class yuppie-junky, a more common breed than many of us are aware.

The booze and the drugs were destroying her health and no one appreciated it more accutely than her. She had come very close to suicide on at least two occasions when in a crisis mode. She had tried drying out, anti-addiction cures and everything else to shake off her dependency, but the one aspect of her life which was always present was her gender dysphoria lingering like an ever present shadow. Because it had not been dealt with, dealing with her other problems became an uphill battle all the way.

The moment she decided to deal with her gender dysphoria in a meaningful planned way, she felt an improvement. The urge for alcohol was eventually contained through Alcoholics Anonymous and the need for drugs was shaken off. She looks 100 per cent better than she was even several short months ago. She is thinner than she was, the bloated look has given way to a more cheerful chubbiness, her skin looks healthier and overall she has a glow which is good to behold. Her last full medical examination pronounced her in good health in every way when only two years earlier she had been given the most serious of warnings by her physician that all her vital signs pointed to an early death unless she mended her ways.

There has been a price. Her domestic issues still remain to be settled, she has challenges ahead in terms of employment, but she is tackling them with gusto and in a most positive manner. Not too long ago she was a candidate for kidney or heart failure and an early berth in a morgue. Today, following a successful surgery, her life expectancy has in every likelihood increased by a good many years.

This once again is the essence of being a transsexual. Beyond a certain point, nature in some way decrees that you have to go into the pit. Then the drive for self-preservation or survival forces you out of the pit, never to be quite as you used to be, but as a renewed and better person with new hopes and new ideals to push you forward. I refer to this as the point of inevitability: you have no control to arrest it, it is not negotiable in any way, and it becomes as pointless to try to resist it as legend says King Canute tried to order the incoming tide to turn about and go out.

* * * * *

I have set out these two examples, of my friend and myself, to try to emphasise the full extent of Kathy's dreadful problem. At one time life looked very black for me, but while everything is relative, my experience and the experiences of others I know pale into insignificance alongside her situation.

In Chapter Five she started off with the year 1970, but it took many more weary years for the official view of her illness to come more into line with the established facts of gender dysphoria.

In telling a little of my own story and that of my unnamed friend I have tried to get the point across that when being buffetted along in a gender dysphoria crisis one tends to lose control of much that is valued and in some cases almost everything and everyone in one's life. The common recourse is to grab at anything which gives relief from the chronic anxiety and stresses which outflow from the condition. So what do you do? My friend turned to alcohol and drugs. I turned to heavy drinking bouts and overeating although I never became alcoholic, but I forgot the principles of good personal management I had always worked by, thus compounding my difficulties. Kathy, with her limited education, ran away from life in a different way—she went on the street, she fed herself and her anxieties by stealing, she became trapped in drugs, and bank robbery was the apparent answer to support her habit. As she gained education within the system she also developed a better understanding of her difficulties, but no one wanted to listen. Typed as a hardened criminal everyone in any authority was only too ready to assume that in some way she only wanted to put one over.

She mentions being judged insane and being sent to Riverview Mental Health Hospital. Here a Dr. Brown referred her to the B.C. Pen psychiatist, a Dr. MacD. When Kathy eventually spoke up and described the nature of her gender dysphoria, Dr. Brown had responded with: "You are not the only one." I may be wrong but that seemed to clearly imply that he had some understanding of the condition having met it before and when she was referred to Dr. MacD. she was likely quite buoyed up.

Dr. MacD.'s remedy was to give her a shot of LSD25 with the comment: "This will make you feel better." One wonders what the doctor might have had in mind for an encore! This was of course the period when Dr. Timothy Leary, the lord high priest of mind-expanding drugs was pushing LSD as a cure-all for many things. Maybe at the time it was thought that it might help gender dysphoria cases, but questioning by myself in medical circles gives no hint of its use today or at any time previously in dealing with this condition. In the fairly extensive literature I have read on the subject I have never come across any reference to the usefulness of LSD. Maybe because Kathy was a prisoner and had no choice within the system she was looked upon as fair game for experimentation. Today, I believe that prescribing LSD when well-known and understood medications are available would go down as malpractice.

Those of us who have our liberty readily forget the priceless privileges we enjoy as common citizens. One such privilege is the freedom of choice. If one goes to the doctor and does not like his attitude, or disagrees with his diagnosis or feels that he is falling short in some other way, then another doctor can always be consulted. It was not so with Kathy. With as little ceremony and no more finesse, she was culled out of the prison population, rather like a steer from a herd for branding. No choice, no debate, no recourse and virtually no appeal, the branding took place with whatever the doctor wanted to apply and she was shoved back into the population. No wonder there are regular suicides within the prison system and no wonder she tried all of six times to end her own life.

There must be punishment to fit the crime, but hopelessness should not be tied to it also, particularly when so much of it is avoidable. Without hope there is no real chance of rehabilitation. Yes, we know there must be rules of conduct and suitable protocols in prisons, but does this have to also include wooden-headed denial in the face of all argument, all reason and common considerations of humanity. The accumulated evidence which we draw upon tends to support the thesis that such wooden responses and callousness created cruel and unusual punishment for Kathy Johnson, quite over and above what she had to serve by way of time.

* * * * *

Chapter Ten

Some Outside Opinions

As I write these words I am thinking of the recently read *Line Screw,* by J. Michael Yates. Mr. Yates is a well-known and competent author with a broad spread of published books to his credit. This book carries the lengthy subtitle *My Twelve Riotous Years Working Behind Bars in Some of Canada's Toughest Jails.* His book is a graphic description of life in the prison system as seen through the eyes of a prison guard. To say the least, the language of communication is not for those with overly sensitive reactions, but from what Kathy tells me her view of life within the prison and the conclusions of Mr. Yates agree on most issues.

There is one variation however, and it tends to confirm our statement that there is a general and wide misunderstanding of what transsexualism actually is and nowhere was this misunderstanding more widespread than in the prison system. In his narrative he describes a drag queen whom he calls Sherrin who, it seems, is quite free with her favours. The story indicates that Yates, to his credit, did not have a rigid reactionary attitude to these people, in fact he found them quite interesting and evidently also amusing when he was doing duty in their area of the prison. With considerable humanity and much common sense he describes a scene on pages 119-120 in his book and I quote:

> *I should explain that while certain guards seem (or pretend) not to be able to handle drag queens, on the*

*tier (and on the street) they are treated with the greatest
of deference. He who manages to capture the attention
and services of a drag queen is one who is held in high
esteem. If he shares his transsexual paramour with the
rest of the tier he is held in the highest of all possible
esteems. Pimping, in and out of jail, is virtually
irresistible. Two walls are available for stacking decks
of tailor-made cigarettes, and I have seen them quite
literally stacked from floor to ceiling with packages and
cartons of cigarettes in the cell of an enterprising drag
queen with an attentive pimp. I was privileged to see
one marriage on the tier (without benefit of chaplain,
but nonetheless solemn and sincere). She got out before
he did (having gone on to federal); the last I heard she
was living in the Fraser Valley outside Vancouver so as
to be near the husband, who was in Kent Penitentiary.*

*This may seem like sexual custom from another
planet. Perhaps this is a comment on me rather than
society in general or the prison population, but I found
the ceremony just as moving as any I ever saw in the
usual places in society.*

*We all have certain needs for bonding, contact and
sex; why should anyone sentenced to time not have
similar needs? At what point do we delimit our
parameters of "punishment"? If we cannot starve
prisoners because of UN guidelines, how can we deny
them other appetites? Is one more important than the
other?*

*Oakalla turned a blind eye to "guerilla sex";
Vancouver Pretrial, where I worked later, went out of
its way to pretend that the sex drive did not exist: it was
a chargeable offence for more than one con to be in a
room at once; therefore there were many dry hands and*

requests for hand-lotion from the nurse after a racy movie. Blue magazines were forbidden. When will we learn that certain things cannot be legislated whether by statute or standing institutional order? The inconsistency between Oakalla and Pretrial (both supposedly maximum institutions) was outrageous. The reason cons view the system as arbitrary is that it is indeed arbitary. His needs, nay, human nature, are rarely considered in the Brave New World of Corrections.

Yates refers above to *his transsexual paramour* and this is where he perhaps unintentionally contributes to the germ of misunderstanding. Drag queens occupy a distinct role within the gay scene as they themselves are usually gay. Often they are club performers or entertainers and as gay men there is usually no interest at all in the considerations or mores of what drives a transsexual. If a drag queen wishes to change sex, which I suggest is usually improbable, it is for some other reason than the deep burning desire which motivates the transsexual who feels and likely has always felt the discomfort of being cast in the wrong gender role. There is an exception, i.e the gay man who under the influence of gender dysphoria sees himself as being philosophically female with a female gender core. After gender change such a person would become heterosexual and would focus on heterosexual males, in what would be a fully normalized relationship. I dealt with this subject in Chapter Eight.

Yates is correct when he addresses the issue that follows in italics. *When will we learn that certain things cannot be legislated whether by statute or standing institutional order?* Exactly; among these certain things is transsexualism. Being a natural even if abnormal condition, it is as senseless to deny its existence as it would be to deny a case of pneumonia. And yet many do, including the prison system, some doctors and religious fundamentalists, all acting as judges on high. Every event in the history of Kathy Johnson as it relates to her transsexualism was subject to denial at virtually every level. Would we deny the case of pneumonia when we stumble across a suffering person? Would we assume that such a person needs no help, no care or medication? The questions answer themselves.

I cannot claim unlimited experience with transsexuals, but from what I can determine a majority come from the ranks of heterosexual men. None are ever glad they are transsexual, probably all over a considerable period have tried to fight it back into the closet of the mind, but usually they are glad they have dealt with it when their transition is completed. The last thing that any one of them ever want to do is ape a drag queen as that is usually the preserve of the transvestite.

There is one group exception. They are the female impersonators who quite often have an honoured role in the theatre, usually as comedians or in some character role which they play. Many well-known, 100 per cent so-called red-blooded males have played a female role at one time or another such as Cary Grant, Jack Lemon, Tony Curtis, Bob Hope, Dick Emery, Dame Edna Everage and so on. What their sexual drives might be in private life in most instances is unknown or not clear, but entertainers in this medium usually keep their private lives and public roles quite separate.

Appearing in drag does not make a person either a transsexual, actual or potential, a drag queen or transvestite, and realistically many, many men have gone to costume parties in drag and thoroughly enjoyed the experience even if they keep rather quiet about it.

Drag, incidentally, is an interesting indicator of an aspect of human nature which affects most people in some way or another. Those who indulge in it do so because fundamentally they enjoy it. Many others who do not indulge in it still enjoy it as a spectacle and for them it might also be a turn-on. At the other end of the scale there are those who abhor it on religious or prejudicial grounds. I doubt if there are that many people in the middle ground who are totally neutral, who have no emotional response to it and whose excitement or anger impulses are not stirred just a little. It's a manifestation of human sexuality by which the male in particular is turned on by borrowing from the female lifestyle. It's a sort of forbidden fruit which for some may carry with it the superstitious threat that those who dabble in it might by some process of black magic be turned into women. I suppose it's a little like the child playing with fire and seeing how far he can go short of burning his fingers. Women don't find a need to go to such preposterous lengths either as "drag kings" or comedians in imitating or lampooning the male element in the population, but they often get a good laugh out of the male performer imitating them in a ribald way.

The foregoing has little or nothing to do with transsexualism. Very few really can correctly define a transsexual. Others, for reasons of pure prejudice, deliberately distort the real meaning of the word, typically mixing such understanding as they have with such other types as drag-queens. I gave an explanation of transsexualism and the needs of the transsexual in Chapter Eight, but here once again we find a well-meaning author confusing the transsexual with other sexual derivations. I can't blame Yates in any way, as it happens every day at all levels of society.

Here is another example in the well-known PBS series *Fame in the Twentieth Century* where Clive James, the commentator, refers to singer David Bowie as being a transsexual, presumably based on the fact that Bowie as a performer paints his face in a grotesque half-woman, half-African witch doctor manner. Whatever Bowie may be I am certain he is not transsexual! In most instances these mistaken identifications are not the end of the world, but for the transsexual seeking normality in terms of her new sex role they are a never-ending source of aggravation and frustration.

* * * * *

What possible mistake could the prison system have made in dealing with Kathy? Was she a drag queen? If she was, she must surely have been the most reluctant one ever in the prison system. Was she a gay man available to all? If she was, she certainly behaved in a manner quite untypical of this type. Was she a simple crossdresser or possibly an exhibitionist as with some transvestites? I doubt that anyone who simply enjoyed dressing up would do it at such incredible risk to her own safety.

What was her purpose then in insisting on dressing within the prison system? I suggest, and she agrees, that it was for the purpose of making her feel comfortable with herself in a female role, the only role she really could play in view of her philosophical view of herself. What did the self-mutilation suggest? Very clearly that she was one of that relatively rare group within the gender dysphoric community who classified as a high intensity transsexual. When the condition becomes so intense that there seems no alternative to self-castration or removal of the penis, other than suicide, then there can be no doubt that the urge is all-consuming, overriding all else in logic.

Here once again we find a lay person, the classification officer Vasha Starry,[4] a man in a position where he has to use some pretty fine judgement, seeing something in Kathy which raised his interest sufficiently to recommend a visit to the prison psychiatrist. A good medical practitioner knows that lay people and patients alike have a point of view which should be taken into account and listened to, but once again we see her hopes for reasonable treatment in depth dashed to pieces. In fact as we shall see it was not until 1980 that something more positive was done,[5] and even then it was filed and largely ignored for a good many years thereafter.

There have never been many transsexuals in the Canadian prison system at any one time. It can be argued that there are too few of them to ever be regarded as any sort of an issue, but it would not matter if there was only one; our system of justice and the treatment of offenders is claimed to be universal in its concept and that one person is accorded the same level of justice as anyone else (which Kathy received in her sentencing) and an adequate level of care for her needs while incarcerated (which she did not receive), whether it be in allowing for a congenital heart condition, a broken leg or an attack of gallstones. She did receive the necessary physical attention after one of her suicide deeds was done, but would it not have been far better to have gone to the source which was causing this constant rebellion? That would have been far too simple, and also it might be added, far too economical for the official Canadian mind so used to wallowing in the trough of public money.

Why should the treatment of gender dysphoria be regarded as an exception to the norm? If a prisoner developed an

---

[4] See Chapter Three

[5] See the *Watson/Diewold Report* of 1980 in Chapter 13

acute heart condition would a general practitioner in the system have handled the matter or would the prisoner have been sent to a specialist? Obviously a specialist would have been called in. Why then, when a relatively rare and unknown condition such as gender dysphoria in its acutest form shows up, does a practitioner unskilled in these matters simply pronounce on it as though he was looking at a dose of flu? "Here, take these three times a day, stay warm and drink lots of fluid." That was about the level of inappropriate response when suggesting yet again to the patient "You will grow out of it" or "It is just a passing phase." If they knew anything about the subject of transsexualism they would know that it is no passing phase, it is a lifetime condition.[6]

There is another matter which needs further elaboration. Kathy refers to developing a relationship with certain protective men including Joe, a repeat offender who is in for life. For a naturally feminine person, further feminized by hormones which she had been obtaining from the outside, it was completely reasonable that she would seek a protector if only for security purposes and that in turn a strong man like Joe would be attracted to protecting someone weaker than himself.

I draw the reader's attention once more to the fourth paragraph in the quote above from J. Michael Yates' book *Line Screw*. In this paragraph Yates states that we all have a need for bonding, contact, sex etc. and in well-chosen words wonders why the system should not expect inmates to be just like anyone else in these important areas of our lives. He pointed out that just as the United Nations prescribes minimum levels of sustenance for prisoners under international standards and then questioned

---

[6] Documentary evidence of much of this will be quoted in Chapter 13 as quoted from official memoranda from 1980 on. At this point we are approximating to 1976 in Kathy's story.

why should it be any different when addressing their sexual appetites.

It is a fact that some prisoners take on the apparent features of the gay lifestyle, but immediately revert to normal standards of heterosexuality upon release. Kathy's need was not for sex in reality; it was a matter of personal security, but she appreciates that it will automatically be concluded by some that both she and Joe were gay. She was not gay and nor was Joe, but both had a need for some mutually empathetic company while they were imprisoned for long periods of their lives. What is a person supposed to do? Perhaps take on the lifeless features of a piece of carved wood! Let's not be ridiculous; these people are living human beings with all the emotions and responses we all have and their needs for friendship, security, and the warmth of human company are not diminished by imprisonment.

In Kathy's case there were long periods when she could only find this security by herself in a segregation unit which she chose in preference to being in the general population. One wonders how a deeply perceptive, conscientous psychiatrist would have seen her and how he would have interpreted this need for security through segregation, in total some 13 years out of her total prison time of 30. Would he have written her off as a loner or would he have seen her as a person in so much danger that anything was preferable to being out in the general prison population? I think an experienced gender dysphoria psychiatrist might just have combined this need for security with the signs thrown off by her attempted suicide record and concluded that both were symptomatic of her deeper need to radically change everything about her physical and mental well-being.

To willingly choose segregation raises another point which can be combined with Yates' comments about human company. Corrections Canada has an attitude that the prisoner at all times must be compliant and well-behaved. If there should be a word of complaint or protest then it could result in a spell in the hole or segregation which amounted to the same thing except that conditions in the hole were even worse than in segregation. Isolation is the principal factor in both cases and it has been the subject of much criticism in individual author's writings and official enquiries. There will be more on this subject in Chapter 12, but in the meantime it is sufficient to note that to deliberately choose segregation as a means of ensuring personal privacy and security must be regarded as an act of supreme desperation and frustration.

Another matter for elaboration concerns Kathy's marriage in 1970 following release from prison. Kathy was obviously still a functional man despite the workings of her mind. Also to that point she had not self-castrated herself. Gender dysphoric people will sometimes refer to dumping all their collection of female clothing in a fit of purging their guilt-laden secrets. In a similar way they will sometimes see marriage as a way to submerge their female selves and without question this sometimes succeeds to a point. They are able to lead a "normal" life with a responsive woman partner and have children.

Unfortunately marriage does not always succeed. Transsexuals suffer from deeply repressed sensitivities which can upset their best plans for a happy future. A weak libido is often one consequence and that would inevitably lead to frustration for both partners. A return of the need to express oneself through crossdressing may be another. Possibly more frequently extraordinary influences unassociated with gender dysphoria tend to undermine the marriage.

My first marriage ended as the result of great selfishness from which I was the victim. In the second marriage the most important culprit was extreme religion. Both were extraordinary influences with which, given my own sensitivities, I was poorly equipped to handle. My lengthy first marriage produced two children with whom I still enjoy a close relationship. I never went into either marriage with other than the intent that it would succeed. I went through some grinding periods of unhappiness so that eventually dealing with my ever-present gender dysphoria looked very compelling. As my life has turned out I have had no important regrets, because having already been to the edge of suicide myself, life now looks very attractive as an alternative to being tied to a loveless marriage or worse still, dead by my own hand.

* * * * *

Chapter Eleven

Weird Trash

If a transsexual person who is not in prison seeks treatment, it is available, although searching it out might be fraught with much difficulty, particularly if the person concerned lives in a more remote community. However, two gender dysphoria clinics operate in Montreal, with one each in Vancouver and Toronto. It is reasonable to hope that others will set up in time in other major Canadian centres, as more medical professionals take an interest in gender dysphoria.

Even if a clinic is not near at hand, knowledge now has improved so that in many instances a local psychiatrist and general practitioner can handle cases with psychiatric and endocrinological advice from specialists perhaps located at one of these clinics.

When a crisis occurs in the life of a transsexual person he may feel impelled to do something about obtaining advice or treatment. This crisis often seems to be the trigger which changes the lives of both the sufferer from the condition and significant others in his family. Such a crisis sometimes leaves a person struggling as though drowning as he tries to deal with a myriad of problems which all seem to be closing in at the same time. It is a crisis of conscience, identity, perceptions, values, ethics, feelings and emotions. One becomes sensitive about things which never shook one's sensitivities before and overall it is possible to suddenly find that everything which was important before becomes unimportant or less so and new considerations dominate one's life.

Now, to survive and even eventually rebuild and prosper again requires a warm and positive climate for new, better trends to take hold. One knows instinctively that things in one's life will never be quite the same again, so it becomes a matter of adjusting to a whole new personal spectrum of values, interests and anything else which will involve a renewed and hopefully improved new life. When my own crisis of confidence and gender identity developed I needed more than anything else to reach out to people who would show understanding and support. I found it at my clinic. My experience was that, for the most part, humanity linked with compassion and an unhurried but knowledgeable understanding were the ingredients I needed while I fought to get a handle back on to my life. While the doctors were getting to know me I was also getting to know my new emerging gender character. I knew it had always been there, but was now graphically more present, rather like a mountain top suddenly free of the clouds which perpetually shrouded it.

Had I not met up with the clinic with its climate of understanding, I honestly cannot think what I would have done at that time. I was near suicidal for a period and the last thing I wanted to meet up with was an unheeding medical practitioner. I did not need to be punished, I did not need to be ignored, and above all I wanted to be heard with the impression that I was getting through. I worked outside the city at the time and could come into town only once per week. Those trips and a weekly visitation to the clinic became vital in enabling me to relate to other people who either had similar problems or at least, as with clinic staff, were available for me to lean on.

As I found my way through this deep shadowed valley of my life, friends I know have said to me on a number of occasions when talking about my experience that they wish I had mentioned it to them sooner as they might have been able to help. Their hearts were in the right place, but their knowledge was zero and I first had a lot to find out about myself and life's values. It did not need a situation akin to the blind leading the blind, but later on when I was ready and armed with an adequate understanding I was able to discuss my situation openly and honestly backed by firm knowledge, and this was far more effective than anything which could have been achieved at the outset.

Another factor which helped me materially was that I was under no pressure applied by any outsider. I was not channelled or programmed in an artificial way. I could get it all out naturally; in fact the clinic created the climate which enabled me to develop my thinking for myself. The staff are there to give advice and no one would lean over any desk and give me a slap in the face figuratively or in fact, as happened on one occasion with Kathy. Even though I needed help and lots of it, I remained my own master at all times. My obligations to the clinic were primarily to keep my appointments and simply follow the ordinary rules of behaviour which would be normal in any clinical climate. When I went on medication I was expected and did follow the prescribed dosage exactly, but if I wished to raise a query on this or any other matter, I was free to do so and then I would be given a proper explanation, and if I needed help by phone I could get it.

It all amounted to highly critical, informed management. It was not enormously complex and nor, I suspect, likely to increase the national debt in terms of cost. The Gender Dysphoria Clinic functioned as part of the Vancouver Hospital Department of Psychiatry and most staff are members of the U.B.C. Department of Psychiatry. It was and remains research oriented and its facilities could be duplicated elsewhere. With proper arrangements and adequate financing, both it and the other clinics could be extended to more fully serve the needs of transsexuals in the prison system.

* * * * *

Contrast the foregoing with the situation that Kathy found herself in. Cut off from the outside throughout most of her period of crisis, she had few people she could rely on to discuss her problems; one or two friendly cons, probably a mere handful throughout the whole of the period. Beyond these there were few she could trust. She was in a snake pit, a savage world as we have seen, peopled by victims and predators and so often the supervisory staff would turn a glassy unseeing eye on the deeds of some of the inmates until the act was done.

When she was able to obtain an appointment with a doctor it was too often a matter of sweeping it all under the carpet. After all, convicts were at the bottom of the social totem pole, perhaps on a par with certain other minorities such as street sex workers, poor deprived women and certain Native Indians. Why should a prisoner expect to receive the same treatment as a wealthy professional or business person. After all, the free and wealthy man and his family had freedom of choice and the economic clout to ensure that he received preferential treatment.

In twice as many years she had a half dozen appointments with psychiatrists. At best, they were always hit and miss affairs. She mentions in Part One having an appointment with a prison pyschiatrist in 1978 who promised to contact medical practitioners. She left his office with a little hope, but it was not until 1980 that an appointment resulted and again after she had done something dramatic which forced attention; in this instance self-castration. Would I as a free person on the outside have had to wait that long for help in the case of my own gender dysphoria? Of course not and I would certainly not have had to self-castrate in order to gain attention.

Admittedly in 1973 when I first decided to investigate the possibilities of treatment I was free to call a well-known clinic in New York from whom I received some free advice which enabled me to plan my next move. I did not act on it as I married again in the classic way of heterosexual transsexuals, who having found a new life partner decided to give marriage a second try in the hope that a happy relationship would once again submerge the condition. When I sought medical advice afresh in 1988 there was little delay in obtaining it, and in early 1989 at just about the worst time in my personal crisis, I obtained a timely entry into the Vancouver Hospital Gender Dysphoria Clinic.

Contrast that once again with Kathy's situation. Can there be any wonder that she suffered severe depression? Can there be any wonder that this depression was at least in part caused by the sense of abandonment which she went through? Can there be any worse feeling than not being in control of your life, always watching and waiting for some positive responses from people who have control of everything? It put one in the same position as a starving animal, waiting, hoping and if lucky being tossed an occasional scrap of food, except that in her case it all came under the heading of emotional sustenance. To my mind it must have been every bit as frustrating as awaiting the rains in a drought stricken desert while life all around crumbles away, including one's own.

One matter which could be aired was her rights under the Canadian Charter of Rights and Freedoms contained in the Constitution Act of 1982. Nowhere have I been able to find that her rights are diminished in the expression of that act. No one doubts that she received fair trials, but what happened after? Was she not entitled to equal and fair treatment, free of cruel and unusual punishment, as with any other citizen? What about the

Federal Health Act? Does this not guarantee equal access of all citizens to health facilities? I find no hint that her rights are diminished in terms of health care. Why should the prison system be empowered to assume that it can handle its prisoners any differently? This perhaps did not apply to fully understood medical conditions, but by what right did the system assume that there should be different considerations when dealing with its transsexual prisoners? Human rights legislation was in being in 1980, but if this legislation was applied retroactively there would have been a clear contravention. As a transsexual Kathy evidently had no rights other than to be treated as some sort of weird trash while within the prison system. The position of the prison management consistantly required that she await her release to the outside. In other words, there was no action to ameliorate a recognised medical condition. If such negativity only provided the fuel for further protest and intransigence on the part of Kathy, then so be it. Any action on her part would have been shrugged off as being entirely of her own doing.

Above all, where was the reasoning intelligence on the part of prison doctors? Did not her persistent and near successful suicide attempts ring some alarm bells? After all, cutting one's jugular was hardly the act of an exhibitionist such as a token cut of the wrist. Near severance of the penis and carefully executed self-castration hardly strikes one as the acts of a happy well-balanced person. The truth appears to be that, then and now, education and therefore the expertise of the so-called experts in various branches of government service seem to be severely lacking. False judgements are rendered by these so-called experts with a levity that makes one shudder.

Transsexualism is too often dismissed as a psychological aberration and is too infrequently recognised as being positively a definable medical condition which brings its own lifetime history like very few other human conditions. In a human rights submission which I recently made on behalf of the Zenith Foundation to the B.C. Human Rights Review, I noted that, in the experience which others and myself had accumulated, the biggest single factor in sustaining ignorance of this condition was to be found in government itself. Civil servants are empowered to exercise judgements without really knowing upon what they are passing judgement.

We already have the evidence of the manner in which British Columbia's Social Credit Ministry of Health embargoed transsexual surgery in 1986 and how the current New Democratic government begrudgingly brought back partial coverage in 1993. A research project undertaken on behalf of the Zenith Foundation in 1994[7] compared the treatment of transsexuals on a province-by-province basis and found that in spite of the so-called equality provisions of the Federal Health Act, treatment from one province to another varied widely. This particularly applies to transsexualism. One wonders if the meaning of the word equality has any significance in terms of transsexualism and its treatment.

Incidentally this study brought out other evidence of ignorance at the level of officialdom having charge of the sector dealing with transsexualism. It is almost laughable as evidence of appalling ignorance on the part of a health official who referred to those "who practise transsexuality" as though it was a witch doctor type ritual, or some remote and nefarious practice. Apart from the fact that the correct word is "transsexualism," we don't "practise" any such thing. By nature's process it finds us in the earlier stages of pregnancy and unfortunately those of us who are

---

[7] A Comparative Study of the Conduct of Provincial Health Ministries in dealing with Gender Dysphoria Cases, Andrea Richard, B.Sc. (Zenith Foundation, 1995)

touched by it have no recourse against anyone or anything. We either endure it if we can, or face the music and deal with it as a fundamental health issue.

Human rights legislation is the area where progress is most likely to be developed in recognising the true elements of transsexualism and the protection of people who suffer from the condition, particularly in the difficult pre-operative transitional period. Transsexuals can recount numberless slights and insults based on pure ignorance and a form of prejudice which is about as evil and ill-conceived as anyone can meet anywhere.

Typical would be such remarks as "There is no place for people like you here." The benefits of the Human Rights Acts, cumbersome though they may be, show through and it is sometimes possible to demonstrate that the offending party has broken the law in such matters.

In certain countries transsexualism merits a legal definition which is enshrined in law. This has the benefit of protecting the transsexual person while in the transition stage in particular, as of course he or she has not yet reached the stage when, as in Canada, re-registration under provincial Vital Statistics Acts is possible. Once this re-registration is complete, legal change becomes a fact. Even though I was born male and have spent most of my life as such I am now legally a female in terms of Canadian law, and again legally cannot be denied any benefits of being a woman. Conversely I also inherit most of the disadvantages. Just the same I believe that a legal definition, probably based on the medical definition quoted in Chapter Eight but extended to set out the rights, protections, duties and obligations of a transsexual while in transition, would be beneficial and would cut out much of the ceaseless raving which originates from some quarters. With a proper legal definition it should also open the way to specified handling of transsexuals in prison.

I have set all this out to illustrate Kathy's unfortunate position, as even today she is not a free agent, being on parole until 1998. However at long last she is free to get on with reorganising her life in terms of gender change. She can now attend the Vancouver Hospital Gender Dysphoria Clinic and hopefully the day may not be too far distant when she can obtain her surgery. She has been approved for it and except for the cost factor the way ahead is simple compared to when she was incarcerated.

But why, when all the facts are considered, would it not have been so much simpler and more economical to have dealt with gender change when in prison? It is a poor excuse to offer the explanation that prisons are not geared up to this sort of procedure. She mentions in her narrative that she wrote to the Hon. Robert Kaplan, then solicitor general and effectively the ultimate head of Corrections Canada, who was surprised to find that Corrections had no policy for dealing with imprisoned transsexuals. He directed Corrections to develop one, but if the civil service do not want to do things it once again proved that bureaucratic footdragging is sufficient to kill a directive. The current policy directive of Corrections Canada is set out in Appendix II. There is every indication that Kathy would have safely and securely settled into the gentler regime of a woman's prison. There would have been a vastly reduced temptation to become involved in further crime. Rebellion was the only weapon she had when she was younger and it did not leave her until she was in her early forties. Today, she is a gentle artistic woman with a good command of the language. Her writing shows real ability and with practice she could become quite accomplished in this field. Her small apartment which is shared by her cat is spotless. I dropped some crumbs one day and before I could reach for them she had cleaned them up. I doubt if one could find a more houseproud woman anywhere. She is a trusted babysitter and loves both children and animals and if things had followed the route they should have in her life she would have made a fine mother, of that I am completely assured.

She makes her first reference to her love for Don in Chapter Six. To sceptics this may sound very improbable, and I know that by the rigid standards of contemporary society it will be dismissed as a simple infatuation between two gay men. They met while in prison and the letter from Don to prison authorities supports the statement that they saw each other as husband and wife as the following indicates:

> *Donald P. B. FPS # 858183A*
> *(name withheld for family reasons)*
> *P.O. Box 880*
> *Kingston, Ont. K7L 4X9*
> *Sept. 10, 1990*

Senior Board Members
National Parole Board
P.O. Box 620
Kingston, Ontario K7L 4X1

To Whom it May Concern:

> *Re: Katherine Johnson FPS #069463A*

I am writing to you in regards to the above mentioned inmate.

As you are all aware, Kathy is a certified transsexual and she is being housed in an all male institution, namely Joyceville. In my opinion, this is cruel and inhumane treatment for her. Kathy and I have been close intimate companions since February 1985 and plan to be together after my release and live as husband and wife.

I am worried and very concerned about Kathy's emotional state of mind at this present time. When she came back to this institution, she was placed on a range separate from me and therefore we seldom see one and other due to the visiting privileges being restricted to inmates living in a different unit and range. Kathy, therefore, has been subjected to a great amount of verbal and physical abuse. Throughout time, living in an all male environment is becoming more and more intolerable for her. She claims to have stressed all of her concerns to her classification officer, Lori MacDonald, and was told by Lori that she can live in the "hole" if she feels so uncomfortable in the prison population! This statement is simply ludicrous, especially coming from another woman! How absurd!

Kathy has asked to be provided with a housecoat for her privacy but has been refused. Her hormone treatment has been cut from 41.75 mg per week to 1.75 mg weekly. Proper medical treatment is just not available to her in prison and therefore she is being destroyed both physically and mentally as each day passes. If verification is required as to her medical treatment prior to her coming to this institution, please feel free to contact her lawyer, Mr. Don Bailey of Mr. Fergus O'Connor's office in Kingston, Ont. Mr. Bailey has a recent letter from Kathy's doctor in Hamilton and it outlines her medical needs. I feel she needs to be back in society as soon as possible so that she can receive her proper medical requirements without delay. . . .

(Signed) Don P. B.

The balance of the letter deals with matters of detail to do with her full parole format and is expressed in such a way as to indicate the deep concerns that Don had for Kathy's health. The response of Lori MacDonald is, as Don suggests, ludicrous, but betrays a mentality which is almost as imprisoned as the prisoners themselves.

Don was not a gay man and Kathy had seen herself as a woman for many years, and that alone was a major root of her overall problem. From what she has told me I have no doubt that there was a genuine and tender love relationship between these two, a circumstance born out by Kathy's gender clinic supervisors who came to know and like Don as a gentleman. Don revered her as a woman and their plan was to see Kathy have her surgery so that the offending penis could be removed and a vagina surgically constructed, and then a proper and legal marriage would have followed. Unfortunately disaster once again intervened as described by Kathy at her conclusion in Chapter Seven.

For the sceptics let me repeat that marriage in a civil ceremony is a legal fact in spite of any argument to the contrary. In British Columbia where Kathy was born, retroactive birth re-registration is provided for in the province's Vital Statistics Act. Providing surgery is complete, has been done by a recognised surgeon and that same has been verified by a doctor licensed to practise in B.C., the subject becomes of the new sex in the fullest legal sense retroactively from birth date. Similar legislation exists in all other Canadian provinces. Inevitable religious ideas to the contrary, this is the legal position.

However there is one caveat. In British Columbia the Vital Statistics Act has never been challenged in court as to the issuance of a retroactive birth certificate and so far as can be determined, nor has it been in any other province, all of which have equivalent legislation. To challenge such a matter there would have to be a reason. If it was challenged it would presumably be based on an allegation of fraud designed to circumvent some other provision of the law.

* * * * *

Chapter Twelve

My Home is Hell

We have become accustomed to seeing the prison as the vindicator of society's collective morality as expressed through the prohibitions of the Criminal Code. For those who dare to attack the security of our person and property, we see the prison as the vehicle for our collective vengeance. Yet, because the prison is the most forceful expression of society's condemnation, it raises the issue of the morality of state power in its starkest form. The prison, seen as the most powerful weapon in our armoury against those who would hurt us, is the part of the criminal justice system that is the least accessible to our gaze and the least amenable to public accountability. What the prison system does, by and large, it does behind closed doors - indeed, doors not just closed but barred, barbed, or encircled by forbidding walls. The prison has been described by one commentator as "the darkest region in the apparatus of justice"; and by another as the outlaw of the criminal-justice system. This latter characterization implies that the prison, as the agent for defending our collective morality as defined by law, in carrying out its task, offends against the law.

So opens the book *Prisoners of Isolation: Solitary Confinement in Canada* (1983) by Michael Jackson. Mr. Jackson is with the Faculty of Law at the University of British Columbia and as a practising lawyer he was well-known as an advocate of prisoners rights. His worthy book ranks as a highly important contribution to the overall body of literature on the issue of imprisonment. It goes into issues which go far beyond anything which Kathy and I wish to touch on here or even have the expertise to assume that we are qualified to do so. However, that takes away nothing in the way of interest in Jackson's book and in the entire subject of imprisonment and its often negative effects. The opening in *Prisoners of Isolation* quoted above confirms much that we in turn are dealing with here.

Historically long-term imprisonment has only been a feature of western ideas on the subject in relatively recent times—say the past 200 years or less. Prior to that prison terms while often harsh in their application were of relatively short term. At one time there were evidently about 150 offences for which one could receive the death penalty, but as ideas on execution have changed so also have prison sentences lengthened. In Canada the frequency and savagery of premeditated and multiple murders have increased the anguish of the public to screaming pitch with backing coming from such national groups as the Union of Police Chiefs. Public opinion polls show that a majority of the citizenry favour a return of the death penalty for certain classes of murder, but the Canadian Parliament in Ottawa consistently relies on the conscience of its members rather than the wishes of the electorate.

One aspect of imprisonment in Jackson's book does have a highly significant bearing on our writings here: the nature of segregation and the "hole" and why both exist. The hole as its slang name implies is just that, a hole used as a means of punishment for wrongdoers who can include everyone from the perpetrators of major prison crimes to those who have committed minor infractions such as answering back or swearing at a guard. Kathy described the hole at Oakalla in the 1960s as being about 6 1/2 ft. by 11 ft. It had a concrete slab on which the prisoner slept without the benefit of bedding and contained a bucket for toilet purposes and a washstand. Above was a single unshielded light bulb which is never turned off so that at whatever angle it is always there to irritate the prisoner. The toilet is in full view of the guard and the prisoner has to lie feet facing the door so that he or she also can be readily seen at any time. The "hole" is not exclusively a male facility.

For food the prisoner was given eight slices of dry bread morning and evening to be washed down by water only. Reading matter was not allowed except for the Bible which Kathy read several times from end to end while incarcerated under these conditions. Sleeping during the day is not allowed, and if a prisoner is found asleep he is hosed down though the grill by a guard with only his own body warmth to dry off his saturated clothing if indeed he is so clad. Ventilation is through a small vent high up out of reach, the result being that there was continuous cold in winter conditions and in summer it became warm and humid, depending on the institution's location.

Segregation was little better. The bed may have wooden slats and mattresses are handed out in the evening and returned to a guard in the morning. For a pillow Kathy placed a roll of toilet paper under her head, but of blankets and sheets there were none. Reading matter was permitted and a half hour of fully supervised exercise took place each day. There was an exception when the segregation was requested by the prisoner or he was placed there for his own protection. In those circumstances he did not lose privileges.

Between the hole and segregation, which in the latter case she requested as a means of obtaining some respite from the constant danger in which she lived out in the population, the longest period in segregation was ten months and in the hole 90 days. Her time in the hole was typically for swearing at a guard which would have ranked as her most serious offence. These minor offences were often deliberate on her part to ensure continuing in segregation even though the conditions were extreme enough to daunt outsiders reading this account. It gives some idea of the choice she felt it necessary to make when considering going back out again with men into the general prison population.

These conditions should not be regarded as exceptional in the system in the period when she was imprisoned and did her last punishment in the hole in 1981, ten years before final release. There may have been improvement in some regards since then, but in general it seems that the higher echelons of prison management did not seem to know too much about what went on below them unless complaints reached their desks. A guard with sadistic tendencies could get away with what amounted to blue murder and all the protestation in the world would fall on deaf ears. She was harassed for about ten years while in Joyceville by a guard called Blakley. She filed a complaint which is in her file. He laughed it off as being "kidding" but was ordered to apologise. He did apologise, but his behaviour quickly became as bad as ever.

Haney Correctional had the unenviable reputation of maintaining the very worst hole in the entire country. Kathy spent about six months in the hole in this institution from 1963-65, not in one stretch but for differing periods. The hole in this case was a bare artificial polished conglomerate stone laid in squares with brass strips in between. The floor was slanted on both sides to form a narrow drainage down the middle. One urinated or defacated into a hole in this drainage channel. The guard would press a button outside the cell to flush the waste material out. The cell was in effect a big latrine. For sleep one slept on the bare stone floor naked and in fact the prisoner was naked 24 hours a day. There was no seat to sit on. If you wanted to sit you squatted on the floor, hemorrhoids notwithstanding. There was a vent in the ceiling blowing cold air at all times. Kathy would lay on the floor with the Bible under her hip and the toilet roll under her head in an effort to reduce skin contact with the stone and it was freezing cold most of the time.

For punishment on one occasion her cell was flooded. Some sort of rubber stopping was placed around the narrow cracks of the cell door and then the flushing valve for the toilet hole was jammed down so that the cell in effect became a huge cistern in which Kathy was trapped like a rat. The guard retreated to his office while the cell filled with very cold water. Kathy is six feet tall. When the water had covered her mouth and was lapping at the base of her nostrils the guard shut the valve off and very slowly the by then roughly 390 cubic feet of water drained out. She was by now suffering from hypothermia and had to be removed to the hospital for four days. If that was not an example of the purest sadism, I have difficulty in thinking of anything worse. She came so close to drowning that it would have ranked as murder in the first degree as it was a deliberate premeditated act. The guard knew what he was doing in trying to break her spirit. There was no question of self-defence, the guard was not attacked or anything, but so far as is known there were no repercussions.

In *Prisoners of Isolation,* Jackson focusses on what amounts to man's inhumanity to man within the prison system. We on the outside have no idea of what goes on inside our federal penitentiaries. It is no solution to say that a prisoner should be locked up "and the key thrown away" to use a popular term, no matter how ugly and extreme his crimes might be. We did away with the death penalty for reasons which have to do with humanity, but in so doing society through our prison system took on the role of managing and supervising the wrongdoer's life. For better or worse we have developed human rights legislation and in the process recognise that because a man is criminal he does not lose his basic human rights which are available to all our citizenry.

However, as noted in Jackson's opening statement quoted above and the quotations elsewhere from Dr. Guy Richmond, quite apart from the writings of Kathy Johnson, it is obvious that the prison institutions in Canada are like indiscriminate meat grinders. God help those who become caught in their coils, their responses can be highly discriminatory or at other times indiscriminate. To the prisoner trapped within there might be hope that just when something positive is to happen, which might assist the prisoner deal with a critical personal problem of whatever nature, it is snatched away again. In the end all that the prisoner has to show for patient waiting and hoping is a mess of frustration.

Jackson's book sets out in detail, far too extensive to quote here, the injustices involved in incarcerations in Solitary Confinement Units (SCU's), such imprisonment being entirely at the whim of the prison management, which appear to have the absolute power of life and death over the prisoner in segregation. Guards can see that a man goes to the hole for the most insignificant reasons and once he is there he can be held indefinitely on the basis of the assessment of management. The reader may remember the threat uttered by a guard against Kathy because she removed her shirt in order to let her skin absorb a few rays of sunshine, "Johnson replace your shirt or go to the hole." On another occasion when in some argument with a female classification officer it was suggested to Kathy that maybe she would like the hole better. That was quoted in Don's letter to the Parole Board also set out in Chapter Seven.

Jackson deals with the case of *McCann v. Her Majesty The Queen & Dragan Cernetic* (1974).[8] In this case Jack McCann, et al, managed to launch an action in the courts following his escape from prison and exposure of the most visible parts of the problem of solitary confinement in the Vancouver newspapers. McCann had the longest record of solitary confinement of any prisoner in the Canadian prison system and this is how he described his years of solitary confinement:

I think treatment in SCU is terrible. I am reminded every day I wake up and when I go to sleep. Men put up there with no concrete reason, no way of knowing how long they'll be up there, no decent answers to questions. No good communication to the classification officer—the lies, the deceit, the stringing along, no one would even be straight with me. The harm it had on others was most affecting on me. It hurt me, I was close to that point myself many times. I had no physical outlet for emotions. I used to break down and cry. Persons mutilating would not even get stitched up by a doctor, just bandaged by nurses and then brought back. I've never slashed up, maybe I am a moral coward, but I want to die my way not their way. . . .

All you live in SCU is bitterness and hatred. For some guys that's not enough. Their hatred reaches the point when they have to see blood, even if it is their own.

Up there I have fears of losing my sanity, fears of losing my friends, fears of myself. There is no physical fear, I can put up with that.

---

[8]   Dragan Cernetic was the warden at B.C. Pen at the time.

In spite of McCann's hatred of blood which he shared with Kathy, McCann could take it no more and finally set fire to himself in his cell. He survived this attempt at self-immolation, but not without the need for extensive plastic surgery on his hands and face.

These remarks were contained in the notes of evidence at the trial. Others were joined with McCann as plaintiffs and the litany of individual experiences cited by Mr. Jackson in the trial evidence is far too extensive to include here. It is sufficient to note all the plaintiffs suffered extensive and aggravated abuse. Some men who were named were in fact driven over the edge into a state of permanent insanity. That is how extreme the conditions were. While I have only read extracts of Alexander Solzhenitsyn's book *Gulag Archipelago* it comes as a real surprise that we have our own Gulags right here.

My point in including these extracts from *Prisoners of Isolation* is to lend additional credibility to the statements of Kathy Johnson. She incidentally knew Jack McCann and counted him as a friend. Mild-mannered and agreeable, he was one of the few she could trust. She remembers him visiting her cell and reading some of his poetry, for he was literate and a good poet. We quote from his poem *My Home is Hell* in view of its topical nature. This has been taken from *Prisoners of Isolation* and was read in court at the trial:

> *My home is hell in one small cell*
> *That no one wants to own,*
> *For here I spend my life condemned*
> *A man the world disowns.*
>
> *So I, the damned, within walls crammed*
> *Live in my man-made grave,*
> *A man all men condemned for sin*
> *But no man strives to save.*

Each lonely dawn that night spawns
I stand and face the wall,
In bitterness and loneliness
I await the whistle's call.

Men scream and yell within my hell
But I'm a man alone,
My tears of pain, like bitter rain,
Spill down on naked stone.

Here every gate is one of hate,
Love has no place to hide
For each lost fool who breaks a rule
The way to hell is wide.

The things men hate and mutilate
Are those that all men value
The mind of man, the wall within
The spirit that God gives you.

The right to sin, but rise again
A free man, not a slave,
To find a friend and at the end,
Escape a pauper's grave.

I cannot tell to those in hell,
The dreams I send above,
Nor how the shrill of whistles kill,
Each passing thought of love.

Within these walls that never fall,
The dammed all come to know,
The row of cells—the special hell,
Called solitary row.

Where seconds cheat and hunger eats
The belly of each slave,

Where gas is shot and each man rots
In his lonely grave.

To sleepless nights, to glaring lights,
To guns and bars and chains,
To walls of stone and men alone,
In years I can't regain.

To those who take my dreams and make
Me live in hell forever.
To those who lash—and try to smash,
The human spirit forever.

To those who steal the things I feel
And sow my heart with sorrow,
Each farewell I bid in hell,
Is lost in each tomorrow.

The harrowing verses of this poem left an impact on me and give pause for thought when we think that the scenes it describes took place every day in maximum security prisons across Canada in the early seventies and prior thereto.

* * * * *

Chapter Thirteen

The Psychiatrists and Psychologists Take a Hand

In 1980 the first intensive psychiatric/psychological assessment of Kathy was undertaken by Dr. Diane B. Watson, then of the Burnaby B.C. Mental Health Unit and Ms. Pat Diewold, registered psychologist at Vancouver General Hospital. In this text this report, which is a cornerstone of Kathy's subsequent medical history, has been referred to as the Watson/Diewold Report.

The report obtained from Corrections Service Canada under the Freedom of Information Act, like other documents referred to or quoted herein, is now set out in its entirety:

> *South Burnaby Health Service*
> *7726 Edmonds St.*
> *Burnaby, B.C.*
> *June 30, 1980*

Dr. Saad
Regional Psychiatric Centre
Abbotsford, B.C.

Dear Dr. Saad:

Re: Douglas (Kathy) Johnson

Douglas, a 32-year old anatomical male and inmate of Kent Institution, was seen on four occasions for psychiatric assessment of his request for sex reassignment. As you are aware he was also given extensive psychological testing by Ms. Pat Diewold, psychologist, who has had considerable experience in this field working with the V.G.H. Sex Therapy Unit. laboratory and x-ray investigations were also performed.

Douglas claims to have had a desire to be a female from a very early age. He shared a room with his sister during early childhood and "always thought we were the same. I played with her friends and can remember wanting to have a doll. My best friend was my teddy bear, I made clothes for it and felt it was my baby." He was placed in Brannan Lake at the age of 10 for incorrigibility and recalls being very frightened of the boys. He felt most uncomfortable in the communal showers and for that reason hated physical education and swimming, hiding away and changing in private as he felt different and embarrassed by the sight of male genitalia. The last 20 years have been spent largely in prison, approximately 13 of which have been in solitary confinement. Douglas claims that he has manoeuvred himself into solitary as he feels uncomfortable living in the male prison environment. In prison he has concentrated on feminine activities of cooking, baking, sewing, embroidery and needlepoint. He took correspondence courses in auto mechanics and wiring which he did not particularly enjoy. He feels that he would like working with children and claims to have very much enjoyed his experience in juvenile counselling.

He claims that prior to 1974 he recognized that there was something very wrong with himself "some kind of freak," but was not aware of the nature of the problem. At that time he read an autobiography of a transsexual and came to the realization that he was a transsexual, certain that a sex change was what he wanted and needed in   order to live a "good, productive life and be happy with myself." He says that despite his awareness of his gender problem he was unable to communicate his feelings to therapists and felt the situation to be hopeless which led to repeated suicide attempts. In 1975 he first acquired estrogens from a physician outside the prison system and managed to get the medication for approximately one year. He claims to have felt more comfortable on female hormones and noted a considerable decrease in tension. When he was no longer able to get the hormones he felt a return of intolerable tension, becoming more depressed as a result. In August 1979 Douglas castrated himself based on the technique he had seen used on steers at Colony Farm. He says he had premeditated the castration as the best alternative if estrogen were not available. Douglas states that it has only been in the last year that he has been able to assert himself in his request for sex reassignment and has been feeling very much more stable within himself, aware of the potential to be helped. He claims to have greatly cut down his use of tranquilisers and no longer feels the need to resort to suicide or slashing. He has started crossdressing to the extent possible in the prison setting, using eye make-up, plucking his eyebrows, wearing "fluffy" sweaters and jewellery. He has the name Kathy labelled on his prison clothing.

The sexual history reveals that Douglas has always had a relatively low libido and sex drive, more interested in the comfort of some passive physical contact. He has had sexual relationships with two women, his wife and a bisexual female friend. He was married in 1970 in an attempt to "prove myself a man," but it was an unsatisfactory relationship which lasted only 13 months. He claims to feel very uncomfortable in heterosexual relationships and attempted to avoid activity to the extent possible. He has an abhorrence for homosexual activity and cannot tolerate a male touching his genitalia. He has had several relationships he considers significant with "straight" men in prison where he played the passive role sexually and felt very contented to cook, clean and care for a "stronger" male figure. Douglas states that he cannot tolerate the sight of his penis and hates having to touch his penis to urinate. He denies any urge to masturbate, denies positive sensations from his penis, and is pleased that since castration he has had fewer erections.

The mental status examination revealed an attractive feminized male with natural female mannerisms and a soft, quiet, passably feminine voice. He was noticeably anxious and obviously eager to please and influence, which is not surprising considering the circumstances. He was extremely well-organized in presenting his case, having a large folder of typed information, including an autobiography and correspondence with FACT (Foundation for the Advancement of Canadian Transsexuals). He was articulate with some tendency towards the dramatic, with rather exaggerated descriptions of his emotional responses. I felt nevertheless that he was accessible and able to establish rapport despite less than ideal circumstances of confidentiality (interview was held with door open in sight of the guards). He seemed a reliable historian with consistency and with no evident attempt to withhold data. There was no evidence of a disorder of mood. There was nothing to indicate thought disorder or an underlying psychotic condition.

His sensorium was clear and intellectual functioning assessed as average. He appears at this time to have fairly good insight into the nature of his problem. His judgement as reflected in his past history has at times been extremely impaired. His personality would be best described as extremely immature with sociopathic tendencies. He has a most stereotyped and passive interpretation of the female role. Laboratory investigations which include a S.N.A 12 and serum testosterone were within normal limits except for S.G.O.T. which was elevated. This is most likely a reflection of soft tissue injury as the other hepatic function tests were not affected. X-ray of chest and skull demonstrated no significant abnormality. Although 24-hour urinary steroids were not evaluated there appears to be no organic etiology to Douglas' gender identity problems.

In summary Douglas presents as a feminized individual who has made a decision that sex reassignment is essential to his well-being, the only alternative being that of suicide. His quest for reassignment has been the sole motivating force in his life, a "fight" that he is not going to abandon but will escalate in intensity should he be prevented from pursuing his goal.

He describes feminine identification since early childhood, but his step-mother and sister, who were contacted by telephone, deny overt evidence of feminization before last year. Neither of these two relatives have been close to the patient so it is difficult to know how much credence should be given to their interpretation that his request is purely an "attention-seeking manipulation." It is certainly possible on the basis of his extensive reading on the subject of transsexualism that Douglas could be simulating a classical history, but it is virtually impossible to prove as the thoughts and feelings involved are highly subjective.

It is definitely the case however, that Douglas has been a dismal failure as a male, committing crimes designed to fail in order to return to the more protective environment of prison. He is indeed a most immature and unstable individual who will have continuing difficulty adjusting to life regardless of sex. It is my impression however, that since making the decision for sex reassignment he has been considerably more stable. He has been receiving a great deal of support from FACT, including offers for jobs and accommodation on leaving prison so it is possible that Douglas has at last found a non-criminal social group where he can receive some degree of acceptance.

I suggest that Douglas be given a trial on hormones and be requested to dress and function to the greatest extent possible in the female role. If there is any ambivalence towards sex reassignment it should then become evident. I suggest that surgery not be considered until Douglas has clearly demonstrated an ability to function with reasonable stability free from criminal activity. I feel there is a definite possibility of rehabilitation in the female role as Douglas has many positive attributes including good intellectual potential, an ability to reason and organize in addition to creativity and sense of humour. He can be a most likeable person if he wants to be. If some steps are not taken towards sex reassignment he will prove an extremely difficult management problem and will most likely be a suicide risk. There seems to be the potential for gain with sex reassignment and as I see it, very little to lose.

The hormone administration should be in the form of Diethylstilbestrol starting with a 5-10 mg daily increasing to 15-20 mg daily if there are no signs of intolerance.

Yours truly,

Dr. D. Watson, M.D., F.R.C.P. (C)
Psychiatrist

DW:ic

Copy: Mr. C. Van de Borne
Kent Institution-Health Care Centre
Agassiz, B.C.

Ms. Pat Diewold's assessment was rendered to Dr. Watson and makes up the balance of the Watson/Diewold report:

June 4, 1980

To: Dr. Diane Watson
(private address deleted by authors)
From: P.A. Diewold
(private address deleted by authors)

Dear Dr. Watson:

Re: JOHNSON, Douglas (Kathy)
Birthdate: April 16, 1948

Douglas, or Kathy as he/she prefers to be called, is a biological male seeking sex reassignment to female. Psychological assessment was carried out on May 16, 1980. Formal tests done were the Shipley-Hartford Test, the Thematic Apperception Test, the Rorschach Test, and the Draw-A-Person Test. A short interview was conducted during the 3 1/2 hour session. For the duration of this report, I will refer to the patient as Douglas since that is consistent with his legal and biological status. However, on other grounds one might make a case for calling him "Kathy" and "her."

Douglas presented as a tall, angular though feminine-looking person wearing eye make-up, having plucked eyebrows, and wearing a jogging suit with a heart on the zipper, the zipper being left a little open. His voice was passably feminine at the low tones in which he spoke. Douglas is 32 and has a (reference is to a word, deleted by Corrections Canada at this point) life history, much of which was in jail. His education was Grade VIII, but he tells me he passed Grade X equivalency exam at Matsqui (Institution). Job training has been within institutions and includes baking and institutional cooking, electricity for the building trades and an auto mechanics course. Douglas did not like electricity but liked auto mechanics a little. He had one year working in the electrical shop but no work experience in auto mechanics although he often visited the auto mechanic shop. He has also taken a "Brain and *Behaviour course" which he liked and a metric course in which he did poorly. Douglas does petit point, embroidery and likes babies. He has artistic interests, wants to study art and wants to improve his grammar through a future course.*

I will discuss some aspects of his life history later after reporting the test results.

<u>*Test Findings:*</u>

On the Shipley-Hartford Test, Douglas obtained a verbal (vocabulary) quotient of (figure deleted by Corrections) bright normal range, and abstract quotient of (figure deleted by Corrections) average range, and a total quotient of (figure deleted by Corrections Canada) average range. The vocabulary part of the test reflects some part of past learning through school, reading and life. The abstract reasoning part of the test reflects current reasoning ability, careful work methods, and flexibility in organizing and reorganizing the elements of each question according to different abstract concepts until the correct organization and concept is discovered, and then the concept is applied. Douglas worked hard and was not impulsive although he would sometimes guess if confused by his deliberations. On the more difficult items, he tried to complicate the task, looking for something more difficult than it was and disqualifying some of his originally correct hypotheses before applying them, that is, he did not trust his own judgement.

On the Rorschach, a relatively unstructured projective test which thus draws upon the patient's way of structuring his perceptions, Douglas showed no abnormal structuring. Most of the responses were popular or nearly popular responses, showing he structures his responses in a way many people do. There is no evidence of psychosis or thought disorder. He was very sensitive to the subtle aspects of shading and to small shaded parts and used these determinants often, a trait reflective of habitual, emotional sensitivity, and showing a tendency to look beyond the surface for subtle details and meanings. In this case, there is not a paranoid orientation to this searching; rather, Douglas appears to feel more comfortable dealing with small details or aspects of experience and while he can also deal with larger parts of his experiences within the environment, there is some tendency when focusing on these subtleties to lose perspective of the other more salient features of environmental experience.

There were a number of sexual responses, mostly vaginas. There is a preoccupation with the vagina, some pleasure was obvious in giving these responses, and an attitude of feminine complicity with me was indicated at times. There are also indications of interest in the head of the penis, perhaps indicating a desire for release of sexual tension at present, but a desire for release of tension does not necessarily indicate much acceptance of such a desire psychologically. Questioning about the "head of penis" response resulted in denial of any association or feeling about this response, either as regards to his penis or that of other men, and he showed much anxiety when questioned. It is possible that the response and the anxiety on questioning may indicate some unresolved conflict about whether he values his penis or not, as a source of sexual pleasure or as some sign of being male, but it is more likely that he is threatened by being a male sexually.

On the Rorschach, Douglas showed a tendency to exaggerate and force some emotional responses by his words and also in the forced use of colour. This is a tendency often seen in somewhat immature persons and reflects anxiety about and difficulty in dealing with feelings.

On the Thematic Apperception Test, Douglas used many of the stories as jumping off points to tell his story. Many characters are sitting and thinking, waiting and wondering. Some of Douglas' characters have high goals for achievement and idealism, but he appears not to consider all of these personal goals but rather a way he would like to think about the world. One is a great musician, one girl goes to college and helps people in society. Another lady with whom he appears to identify designs clothes and manufactures them successfully. Three responses alluded to suicidal attempts, two of them women, one not identified by sex but reminding him of one of his earlier attempts. In one story the woman, after such a struggle in life, gave up and shot herself. Douglas related this to himself and specifically to his transsexual desire. He said he felt he was a hopeless case and no one seemed to help. He was so non-assertive in the past he could not speak his mind easily. He also mentioned a 10 1/2 month period in a "deep segregation unit" because he was not comfortable in an all-male environment, all in the context of feeling hopeless and suicidal.

The other suicidal theme with a woman occurred on the so-called "sex card"; again supporting his earlier statements that sexual conflicts were major determinants of suicidal attempts. Douglas had difficulty relating to two cards on which there were father-son and mother-son themes; in each case lamenting the fact there had not been closer relationships with parental figures, father and stepmother. He especially wanted approval from both—the father to have seen him as a "good person for a change" and the stepmother to understand the transsexual desire. Two other stories, which Douglas also related to himself, show pleasure in Douglas' relationship as a female to males. Another card elicited admiration of a muscular type of male physique. Douglas indicated he would not feel afraid of other males if with this man, thus indicating a need for protection as well as attraction to the man, which are factors for him in choosing a male friend.

Douglas indicated that in jail he often feels different and afraid and like he is getting in with a pack of wolves when with groups of males. One other story portrays Douglas' fear of males. In one story, the male is a potential date and the female senses something about the person that bothers her and is feeling afraid of his strength. To summarize the TAT story findings, the stories reflect dependency on others for support and show his needs for acceptance. They show some difficulty in dealing with sad, harsher realities of life and a tendency to be idealistic and naive about levels of achievement and also human relationships. Douglas almost always identified with adult females, but can identify with young boys or with the son in the cards

*where children or parental figures are involved.
Feelings of hopelessness and suicide attempts bring up
past memories which are close enough to be still
painful. No suicidal thoughts appear for the present.*

*On the Draw-A-Person, Douglas first drew a
female, then a male. This is the order usually done by
females. The female had little figure definition but was
in a feminine dress. There were no feet drawn however,
usually a sign of feelings of helplessness. However,
Douglas also indicated he did not know how to draw
feet although he did so on the male. Perhaps some
artistic anxieties were involved. The male drawing had
more shading, especially on shoulders and arms, a sign
of anxiety, perhaps about strength, probably in other
males.*

*Concerning the transsexual issue, the test results
indicate female identification as an adult. Concerning
sexual organ identification, there is much
preoccupation with the vagina, though of course, no
chance to identify with it as a physical part of himself.
However, almost everything he tells about his history
and sexual involvement indicates depressive feelings
about erections and about having to touch his penis
when urinating and trying to avoid sexual activity when
married (1970, 13 months duration) and especially
trying to avoid being on top. He wanted to play a
passive feminine role sexually and also wanted to do
the cooking and housework. Douglas also had a
bisexual female friend and twice they had sex, but
Douglas said he felt depressed after sex with her.*

*He has played a feminine role in relationships with
two or three men in prison. Up until 1974 he thought he
was a feminized male or some kind of freak. In 1974 he*

finally became certain a sex change was what he needed in order to live a "good, productive life and be happy with myself." All his life he said he was feminine. Since he was a child, Douglas said he wished he was a woman. He says he was three years old when he saw his first male child— his aunt looked after him since he was two and a half and he saw his father rarely. When his father told him to play with a little boy who was down the road instead of with his sister and her girlfriend, Douglas was afraid. He said his father tried to pull him to the boy and he "freaked" and ran behind the house. Douglas does not know why he reacted this way. Even at school, Douglas said he played with girls.

The history Douglas gives is consistent with that found in most transsexuals involving wanting to be female, sexual confusion, avoidance of sexual activity as a male partner, and less interest in sex than in being a complete human being of the opposite sex. Despite his decision in 1974, Douglas had difficulty in speaking out for himself, he said. He relates at least some of the suicide attempts to transsexual desires with no hope of being helped. He was happy to be on hormones, but depressed when these were discontinued. About one year ago he castrated himself without anaesthetic. This produced the result of less erections and Douglas says he does not have an urge to use his penis anymore. He is happy not to have the erections but still feels tense to have to touch his penis when urinating. He says as far as he is concerned, he has not got a penis and he notices it only when urinating or in the shower. Douglas has not made suicide attempts recently and relates this to progress on the transsexual route and knowing he will be heard and win. He is also almost completely off tranquilizers in the last while, although he still experiences much tension and also tension headaches.

The history suggests poor adjustment as a male since childhood. If his statement, he wished he were a woman since he was a child, can be accepted, then much female identification has also been present. Now despite some anxiety about his penis, he seems female in thinking, orientation and identification including some sexual identification. Due to Douglas' immaturity, one would expect much difficulty adjusting as a male, but since he has gone so far in the female role and appears to feel happier in it, adjustment as a female seems the only feasible solution. Even without the castration, I would recommend Douglas as an appropriate transsexual (gender reassignment) candidate. The castration, in my mind, removes any chance for successful help toward male adjustment although attempts at making him a well adjusted male would almost certainly be unsuccessful anyway given the long "feminine" history.

Thank you for referring this (next word deleted by Corrections Canada) perhaps now more hopeful human being to me.

Yours truly,

P.A. Diewold, M.A.
Psychologist

cc: Mr. C. Van de Borne
Kent Institution-Health Care Centre
Agassiz, B.C.

Please note that Dr. Watson *suggested* a prescription as a part of her assessment and that both consultants were in agreement in their final conclusions as to the transsexual nature of Kathy. These reports were clearly submitted as recommendations. There was no mandate that either had charge of the patient in the sense of being able to initiate a workable course of treatment. If such were the case, it would have required considerable consulting and supervision outside the prison compound. Both reports were submitted on June 30, 1980, which certainly gave them time for circulation and consideration.

There must have been lots of activity around this time on the Johnson file. On July 9, 1980, Robert B. Cormier, Ph.D., psychologist, wrote a report to Warden Payne at Joyceville. It will be noted that this coincided within days of the receipt of the Watson/Diewold report. Dr. Cormier wrote:

#5526 JOHNSON, Douglas ("Kathy")

In response to your request for an assessment on the above-mentioned inmate I submit the following:

1. JOHNSON believes he is a transsexual, and is committed to changing his body from male to female. To this end he has castrated himself, has taken female hormones, and is currently seeking female hormones at Joyceville.

2. There is a great deal of controversy on the subject of transsexuality—whether it is a bona fide *phenomenon and whether a sex change is an advisable course of action. A well-known clinic at John Hopkins (Hospital, New York) stopped performing these operations a few years ago when their long-term study showed that those who had undergone the sex change operations were no better adjusted afterward than those who had not. However, their selected sample may not have been representative of transsexuals as a whole, and the John Hopkins study is not considered definitive. I understand that the Clarke Institute of Psychiatry in Toronto operates a gender identity clinic, but I am not familiar with it.*

3. In interview, JOHNSON impresses as thoughtful and bright. He has done some study in the area of psychology and biology, and has researched transsexuality through contact with the Foundation for the Advancement of Canadian Transsexuals (FACT). He informed me that he had undergone gender identity assessment with Dr. Diane Watson, psychiatrist, and Dr. Patricia Diewold, psychologist, at the South Burnaby Mental Health Clinic earlier this year while he was a patient at R.P.C. Pacific and that the results of the assessment had cleared the way for hormone therapy. I have not reviewed the medical records that may document this conclusion.

4. I think any attempt to convince JOHNSON to return to a male-orientation would be futile. In his present condition without any substantial secretions of sexual hormones in his body, his sexual identity is uncertain. This uncertainty is contributing to a state of general malaise and tension.

5. In my opinion female hormone therapy would contribute to his psychological well-being, and unless there are clear medical contraindications, should be provided. Of course Drs. Webb and Carpenter could advise you in respect to the medical aspects of this therapy.

(signed) R.B. Cormier

Dr. Cormier's report evidently had no positive impact either on Warden Payne, who understandably relied on his professional advisors, or the senior professional advisor, Dr. Stanley Webb, whose behaviour indicated an attitude of holding the line at any cost. Then we find in the file the following scribbled note dated September 2, 1980:

I am not willing to assume responsibility for side effects from hormone therapy suggested by others who will not order it.

S.W.

The initials appear to be those of Stanley Webb, M.D. Who the "others" are is inconclusive but from the file it would appear that Webb was referring to Dr. Diane Watson's suggestion, as Dr. Cormier's report prescribed nothing beyond recommending that hormones be continued.

Predating this handwritten note is a letter from Claire Culhaine, the well-known Prisoners' Rights Activist, dated August 1, 1980. We quote:

Mr. K. Payne, Warden,
Joyceville Institution,
P.O. Box 880
Kingston, Ont. K7L 4X9

Dear Mr. Payne:
In correspondence with prisoner Kathy Johnson, #5526, I am advised that there appears to be some divergence of opinion regarding the issuance of hormones.
On the one hand the psychiatrist and psychologist agree, but the medical doctor is negating their

recommendation, despite firm representation on the part of Dr. Diane Watson, of Burnaby, B.C., who treated the patient before transfer to your institution, when I was visiting her at R.P.C. (Regional Psychiatric Centre) Pacific.

Would you be good enough to give this matter your personal attention, at your earliest convenience, in order to minimize the problems already present in this particular case.

Thank you for your intervention.

Yours truly,

*Claire Culhaine
for: Prisoners' Rights Group (PRG)*

By letter of September 9, 1980, Warden Payne had the Joyceville physician, the same Dr. Stanley Webb referred to above, reply to Ms. Culhaine:

*Miss Claire Culhaine,
Prisoners' Rights Group,
(Street address deleted by authors)
Burnaby, B.C.*

Dear Madam:

Re: Inmate #5526 JOHNSON, Douglas Melvin

Mr. K. Payne, Warden of Joyceville Institution, has requested that I answer your letter regarding the above named inmate, who you incorrectly identify as "Kathy" Johnson.

It is my professional opinion, and the opinion of other physicians supervising this inmate's case, that female sex hormone therapy in this instance is inappropriate, and we are unwilling to assume the consequences of such unjustifiable treatment based entirely on the demands of the inmate.

Yours truly,

(Stanley Webb) M.D.
Institution Physician

This unsatisfactory reply when set alongside and compared with the Watson/Diewold and the Cormier reports together with Webb's letter to Ms. Culhaine speak for themselves. Webb's reply encapsulates much that is at the heart of the system's failure to adequately respond to what, at this point (1980), has been clearly identified as transsexualism. Webb was not a psychiatrist. To have so cynically contradicted the contents of the reports by other professionals, some of whom had acknowledged expertise in their chosen field, is about on a par with a patient with a fully identified physical problem such as a broken arm having that contradicted by the doctor stating that he is suffering from an abscessed tooth instead!

In truth the evidence that the entire history of Kathy Johnson while a prisoner brings out is that prison physicians did not understand transsexualism and quite possibly even today they are lacking in their knowledge and experience. As to why the sex hormone therapy was "inappropriate" and the treatment "unjustified," as expressed by Webb, was again an expression of an uneducated point of view as there is no professional basis for going against the opinion of recognised experts.

One cannot help thinking that Webb had a severe personal bias against Kathy. Or was it a religiously based bias against transsexuals in general? The small-minded insistence on the correct legal name when replying to Claire Culhaine is an example of this. But worse still is the recollection (see Chapter Five) that it was this same doctor who offered Kathy testosterone shots after she entered Joyceville a short time prior to this episode in late 1980. Kathy had already castrated herself and no matter how one might judge the severity or acceptability of this act against her own person, it is a fact that the natural source of testosterone had been removed. It is inconceivable as to just what degree of extreme ignorance of human endocrine factors and the psychological basis of transsexualism existed with this doctor at that time. Apart from all else why would the prescribing of testosterone be acceptable to the doctor when estrogen was not? There is much that is contradictory here but as the events took place 15 years ago it might all be written off as history. That is except for one factor, the contribution to the wear and tear on Kathy's mind and body and the reason why she now is on a permanent disability pension.

I am a lay person, clearly transsexual, but not subject to the high pressures that affected Kathy on a daily basis. Even I with my limited medical knowledge of the subject can readily appreciate the feeling of hopelessness that this sort of treatment would engender in a high intensity transsexual such as Kathy. Worse than that, the reintroduction of testosterone into a human being who had clearly rejected the hormone like a poison to her system could have caused a whole range of medical complications, physical and mental, when her then current situation was already too complex for any easy answers.

* * * * *

Both of these authors know Dr. Watson and Ms. Diewold personally. They and their colleagues at the Vancouver Hospital

Gender Dysphoria Clinic deal more or less continuously with a range of gender dysphoric cases. The team of around ten professionals are known and trusted by their clients. They blend humanity with compassion, but expressed in the vernacular, "they are not patsies, waiting to be sold a bill of goods." Everyone is dealt with on a cross-referral basis, meaning that every step of the way, each specialist opinion is cross-checked with that of one or more members of the team.

Now admittedly, in 1980 the Gender Dysphoria Clinic did not exist at Vancouver General. In fact the only such institution from Toronto westward was the Clarke Institute in that city. Nevertheless both Watson and Diewold were already dealing with gender dysphoria cases and had been for something close to ten years prior. It can be stated with accuracy that both ranked as experts in British Columbia.

In general gender dysphoria follows a predictable pattern in terms of its origins and the steps that have to be taken by the individual in dealing with it. On a case-by-case basis, matters of detail reflect the differing personalities and backgrounds of each individual and in some instances are made more complex by additional psychological or physical factors. The Watson table (see Appendix One) sets out a broad description of each of the five general classifications of gender dysphoria, but basically we are mostly concerned here with Groups Three to Five. Groups Four and Five are what I personally regard as the "true" transsexuals, but having said that, I realise that some might well dispute my interpretation. All in some manner have a female core identity which, in the mind of the subject person, have frequently, but not always, been consciously present since infancy or early childhood.

As noted in Chapter Eight, strong influences often accompanied by or even precipitated by a personal crisis bring on the conviction in the mind of the subject person that there can be no peace or real happiness until their gender dysphoria is dealt with. Gender dysphoria is always present throughout the subject's lifetime because whatever the treatment, one's fundamental biological sex cannot be reconstructed, which is of course the basis of gender dysphoria, i.e. when the physically manifested biological sex is incongruent with the brain sex of the individual.

On the other hand perceived gender identity can be changed following a generally standardised, internationally recognised procedure known as the Harry Benjamin Standards of Care. As noted earlier these standards provide for psychiatric/psychological examination and ongoing counselling, endocrine analysis, supervised hormone treatment, ongoing medical supervision and if all factors taken together syncronize, surgical amendment of the original and construction of the new genitalia.

Having laid out the fundamentals of so-called sex change, let us try to draw some conclusions on some other aspects of this complex subject. The following incorporates much that has already been touched upon previously and in Kathy's narrative, but will be useful by way of summary:

1) A common misconception is that it is a condition which manifests itself as being something kinky and bizarre. It cannot be stated that kinkiness does not appeal to some transsexuals, but it can also be said that within the general population, i.e. the vast majority who are unaffected by gender dysphoria, kinkiness or the bizarre occurs widely and takes many forms.

2) This is a lifetime condition. Basically, one is born with it and it dies with you. It cannot be beaten out by any method yet devised, including persuasion counselling or physical persuasion as may be resorted to by an overly-zealous parent, as even if it apparently disappears it is fully capable of emerging again if the right combination of stress and anxiety occurs. It should also be noted that it less frequently occurs like a "bolt from the blue" where no stress or anxiety are involved. It also tends to increase in intensity as the subject individual matures and ages.

3) The condition is not unique to homosexuals. While there are no statistics that the authors are aware of, observations and personal contact indicate that the majority are from a heterosexual background, often with marriage and children as a part of their personal history. Whether they remain heterosexual following gender change is a moot point. However, many appear to retain their preference for women and in reality would be reclassified as lesbians if entering into a sexual relationship. Among gays there are those evidencing a female exterior such as drag queens who remain gay as they have no desire to change their genitalia. A gay man normally wants another gay man and the last thing he wants is the loss of his masculine genital identity.

4) There is another variant and that is the gay man with a female core identity. He usually finds that he is not attracted to gay men but is attracted to heterosexual men. His female core identity is what controls his impulses and the remedy for this type is gender change which thus enables him, at least in theory, to fulfil a female heterosexual role and thus unite with a heterosexual man.

* * * * *

Kathy Johnson would, as earlier noted, be classified as a Group Five high intensity transsexual. Had she had a normal upbringing and had her career followed a more acceptable route free of the restrictions of incarceration it may well be supposed that she could have simply developed as a Group Four medium-intensity type. Environmental factors can intensify gender dysphoria, but of themselves there appears no basis to suggest that they will cause it.

However, as we know, neither her upbringing nor her subsequent career were normal and the constraints of imprisonment created many distortions for her. The most critical one was of course her inability to function like other human beings other than those who shared her imprisonment and all this intensified her extreme frustration and continuous disappointment. It can be hardly surprising that she focussed so intensively on her need for adjustment in her life by way of gender change, as she saw it as the one escape route open to her to retreat from the continual cycle of violence, crime, and depravity on the one hand, and official indifference and uncertainty on the other.

The official viewpoint cannot accommodate itself to the fact that she was suffering a double imprisonment; the legal imprisonment imposed by law and the imprisonment of her feminine spirit within the confines of her mind and its need to express itself. In that segregation and the hole are a prison within a prison it could even be claimed that over lengthy periods she suffered what amounted to a triple imprisonment. Oh, yes, we are aware that this last statement will be debunked by the sceptics who evidently fill the ranks of prison officialdom as just so much nonsense, but reference to the official file supports this statement.

In many ways Kathy's life has been one of continuous protest, and though much of this protest might have been the wrong way for the right reasons, it never seemed to occur to anyone, except the psychiatrists and psychologists named here, that the simple answer to creating a more harmonious, happier prisoner was to ease her discomfort by giving her hormone therapy and under proper supervision, ultimately her surgery. If there is a word of advice to transsexually affected people it has to be, "Don't fall into the hands of the law, unless you are prepared for a fate worse than death."

Another major factor was that she was bound by a prison code of secrecy, or avoidance of falling into the ranks of the stool pigeons. This might be interpreted as a sort of honour code, misplaced though most of us would consider it on the outside. It might also be said that an element of pragmatism was applied by Kathy. In reality maintaining the code was motivated by fear, as retribution for those who broke it invariably meant severe injury and even death. Twice while on parole she was innocently caught in situations which brought further imprisonment for her and yet her lips were sealed according to this code. Had she spoken up she might have avoided further persecution and the wrongdoer in both instances would have still paid the penalty earned regardless.

We on the outside might shake our heads and ask why one should compromise oneself by getting into such situations. For a long-term offender the society that such a person develops as a part of his/her life is drawn from within the prison population. These people become one's friends and enemies, and among the friends they are often the only ones to whom a person can turn when in need of the support given by a friend. We all do it in our respective circles, whether it be an old school association, a sorority, a regimental or service association, a club with mutual interests and scores of other alternatives. In prison circles it is inevitable that prisoners take on the hue of lepers, known to be there but not wanted by anyone.

Why should it be any different when the only life you have known has been prison? Kathy went into the system at age 10 with a spell in reform school and up until her final release in 1992 when she was 44, the longest period of freedom she was to know was a mere twenty months.

* * * * *

The Watson/Diewold report apportions no blame. That was not its purpose, but in identifying and classifying Kathy's gender dysphoria in detail it did something to which no other specialist evidently had given serious thought or time up to that date. Hitherto, if she was lucky she got a twenty-minute appointment and a brush-off about on a par with the diagnosis of a minor ailment. Dr. Watson intensively interviewed Kathy on no less than four different occasions, a far better basis for reaching sound conclusions than anything that had taken place in the past.

However, in considering these facts one should read the Federal Corrections directive for handling transsexual cases set out in Appendix II. It is a dry soulless document which falls far short of the Province of British Columbia Corrections directive set out as a comparison in the same appendix. Both speak for themselves. One wonders why there can be such a variation in approach between that of the federal level of government and the more junior provincial level. It might be given as a justification that provincial jurisdiction only covers those situations where sentences do not exceed two years less a day, which obviously can only cover those who commit lesser crimes.

One of the worst shortcomings of the Corrections Canada directive is that it shows no imagination, no inspiration which would lead to a better understanding. It encourages the *status quo* and ignorance, and creates no incentive which would lead a lazy unenquiring professional mind to try to respond better and more constructively to a given medical condition. It presupposes that its functionaries in both the medical and supervisory branches either have a knowledge of gender dysphoria which needs no improvement, or else that the ignorance, which documentary evidence clearly shows, should be allowed to continue to the obvious detriment of a small minority of prisoners. It could be added that there are still medical practitioners who doubt the real existence of transsexualism as a medical condition and refuse to take it seriously, or either condemn it outright as a moral aberration. However, it is encouraging to note that medical schools are now adding the subject to their curriculum for medical students.

The Watson/Diewold report was submitted by Dr. Watson on June 30, 1980, to the person who made the referral—Dr. Saad at Regional Psychiatric Centre, Abbotsford. By the time this report came out Kathy had transferred to the Ontario penal system in the forlorn hope that treatment of gender dysphoria was more advanced than in B.C.

* * * * *

Another important professional report followed the Watson/Diewold report and the Cormier letter. All the reports written with a degree of typical professional caution agree on the need for female hormone therapy. The Morelli report, coming as it did six years later, comments specifically on the trap between maleness and femaleness within which Kathy was caught without seemingly making any progress. What follows must be regarded as an important document as it amounts to a progress report covering the six years since the Watson/Diewold report:

JOHNSON, Kathy (#069463A)

Kathy Johnson is a thirty-seven year old transsexual who has had extensive psychiatric and psychological involvement in the past. Much of this has centred around her transsexuality and in particular her reaction to delays and difficulties encountered in the meeting of her special needs in a male correctional system.

Kathy Johnson was first seen by myself at the Kingston Penitentiary Regional Treatment Centre in the fall of 1980 (please see psychological report dated October 15, 1980). Kathy again returned to this centre in December 1983 and psychological reports are available from this period. After this last return from KPTC, and until his retirement in April 1985, Kathy Johnson was seen by Dr. Montgomery of the Joyceville Institution Psychology Department. Clinical contact between myself and Kathy was reinitiated on April 30, 1985, 13 more sessions followed until March, 1986.

In the past the following psychological difficulties had been noted:

- *depression*
- *agitation and generalized anxiety*
- *low frustration tolerance especially re her treatment as a transsexual*
- *self-mutilation*

During the 11 months that I have seen her and the 14 months prior to that, no instances of self-mutilation have occurred. Compared to the Kathy I knew in 1980, I have been impressed with the gains Kathy has made. Her frustration tolerance has improved in particular and most notably her ability to cope with frustration has improved greatly. In addition, while Kathy is still emotionally labile, as the result of a recent administration of MMPI to be discussed shortly, she is now better able to appropriately cope with these feelings. She is in better control of her behaviour, although she has yet to verbally acknowledge this control. The goal of our sessions was to support and encourage Kathy in her coping efforts and in aiding her to further refine these. In December/85 and January/86, she successfully coped with feelings of depression at the loss of a close friend without experiencing a relapse. This is not to suggest that Kathy's stress management and coping skills cannot be further improved. In addition her communication skills and assertion skills in particular need to be improved, if she is to make necessary gains in social self-esteem and self-efficiency.

These latter changes are felt to be particularly important for Kathy's personal development and ability to independently survive in the community, something Kathy showed herself not yet capable of doing in 1983, at the time of her last short period on the "street." (Author's note: Kathy gave her own explanation of this circumstance in Chapter Six.)

The results of the Minnesota Multiphasic Personality Inventory (MMPI) completed in November 1985 indicated an individual still "crying for help." The picture that emerges of Kathy is of someone who is dissatisfied with herself and her life, who feels socially alienated, feeling different from others and not well understood by others. She is particularly concerned with bodily functions and changes in such, much anxiety being expressed or channelled through physical complaints. In short, while Kathy is now better coping with everyday life issues, much energy and effort is required; life is a strain. In addition Kathy emerged as an emotional, socially dependent person, who is slowly becoming more aware of her ability to control her emotions and emotional reactions, but who has not yet fully realized this. Consonant with her law-breaking past and lifestyle, Kathy's values do not totally mesh with those of society in general.

It is hypothesized that some of the difficulties in personality structure noted at this time may be the by-products of gender dysphoria that Kathy is experiencing, having decided some years ago that "she was a woman trapped in a man's body," but having been unable to accomplish any appreciable progress towards meshing what she feels as her psychological and physical selves. She has been taking small doses of female hormones and been trapped for some time in a limbo between maleness and femaleness and moving towards neither.

Rose Morelli, Ph.D.
Psychologist.

The Watson/Diewold report, taken with the Cormier and Morelli reports, do not specifically criticize Corrections Canada, but in repeatedly hammering away at a similar theme, they do outline circumstances which infer that it is a fundamentally moribund organization, ignorant and abusive in its management role and therefore a body which deserves severe censure and a complete reassessment of its functions in managing the lives of prisoners over which it has total control. Its treatment of Kathy in many ways meshes with the extremes described by Michael Jackson referred to at the beginning of this chapter.

* * * * *

Prisoner of Gender

Chapter Fourteen

"J'ACCUSE"[9]

I become so sick and tired of the afternoon television talkshows and their treatment of frequently sensitive subjects. How they persuade people to appear and talk openly about their deepest emotional problems is always a matter for wonderment to me. If Donahue or Geraldo put on a learned enough look and adopt a parsimonious tone they seem capable of sweating almost anything out of the poor unfortunates with whom they share the stage for an hour. The performance is usually looked upon as entertainment rather than education by the audience, which often follows the subject for discussion with about the same fervour as the massed audience did in the days of the Roman gladiators. I wonder how many of them think that there, but for the grace of God, go I.

Yet in all honesty it has to equally be admitted that in spite of the entertainment value of such shows, they are sometimes the only source of popular education available and

---

[9] Inspired by the title of the book *J'Accuse* (1898) by Emil Zola, noted French 19th century author. Zola wrote this book to describe the lies, prejudices and misrepresentations employed to wrongfully convict French-Jewish army officer Alfred Dreyfus of treason and send him to long-term penal servitude at the feared Devil's Island penal colony in French Guiana. Zola's book created public pressure and won a fresh trial for Dreyfus at which time he was found innocent of all charges.

this applies in particular to the subject of transsexualism. By the admission of Phil Donahue, this is about the most popular subject the talk show industry has yet come across.

Admittedly some talk show hosts do a better job than others, one such being Jerry Springer who conveys a degree of sensitivity which sometimes escapes the others. In a recent show he took the time to give a well-balanced explanation of what transsexualism actually is, getting across the fact that it is of biological origin commencing in the womb and lasting for life, with no cure in prospect in which a complete recovery and non-recurrence can be assumed as with many other human conditions.

On many occasions I have listened to a tirade from a religious point of view. Beating their breasts and tearing their hair out these self-described emissaries of God rant on with exhortations to come to the Lord for forgiveness, with the added prize that all will then be forgiven. I have heard transsexualism described as the grossest of perversions, "condemned in the eyes of the Lord" and yet it is remarkable how many of these bigotted evangelists have skeletons in their own closets. How often does one hear preachings from the pulpit only to find that homosexuality, drug addiction and criminal propensities are just as likely to be found in the family of the preacher or even the preacher himself!

Transsexualism is not mentioned in the Bible although there are references to crossdressing which is not, I repeat, not the same thing. Yet a preacher from the Pope down will take it upon himself to render his own interpretations on many things without reference to established expertise.

How then do civil servants, including prison officials, gain their education in such subjects as transsexualism? Usually it comes from these self-same talk shows or items in the popular daily press. It does not come from authoritative sources as a general rule, although in British Columbia and much of the rest of Canada it is now easy and straightforward for the transsexual person to deal with such items as passports, driving licences, name change, birth re-registration and police matters without suffering abuse or harassment as used to happen years ago. Civil servants are entitled to their own private opinions like anyone else, but it seems obvious that at least in the handling of these relatively routine matters some enlightenment has crept in.

Human rights legislation now exists at both the provincial and federal levels and backing them up as the paramount law we have the Canadian Charter of Rights and Freedoms, all of which tend to serve the free citizen increasingly well, but as the late Dr. Guy Richmond in his book *Prison Doctor* (1975) states, and we quote:

> *Once he enters prison, the inmate loses almost all privileges we take for granted. One of those most treasured is freedom of communication. A prisoner is denied this right. Every letter he writes or receives is scrutinized and can be censored or even withheld. There is justification for this procedure. Illegal drugs are often concealed under a postage stamp, or a letter may reveal the location of a cache of drugs thrown over the wall by a passer-by. Escapes may also be arranged, or a letter may contain distressing news which might result in serious depressions or even trigger a suicide.*
>
> *The simplest requests of a prison inmate can be denied; unnecessary and provocative orders have to be obeyed without hesitation. Even if the prisoner is insulted he must remain silent or there will be a disciplinary report. In all prison staffs there are bound to be members who are not suited to the care of offenders and who make remarks such as, "You're an*

animal and I'm going to treat you as one." There is little to protect a prison inmate from verbal abuse, though I have never served under a governor or warden who would tolerate this if it were brought to his notice. The humanity or otherwise of the head of an institution is reflected right down the line. Misuse of authority eventually defeats itself, and a great deal of suffering can be caused before it does so.

The nature of transsexualism is that it is an abnormal but natural human condition. For the sufferer there is a *point of inevitability* when it becomes imperative to deal with it as a medical problem and seek normalization, sometimes to avoid the alternative of suicide. Until it is dealt with it becomes the transcending challenge in one's existence and to better illustrate this aspect I am setting down a few more details of my own personal life and the challenge I had to meet in order to assure myself of any happiness and security. My life experience has been set in the context of a free citizen, but in Kathy's case quite the opposite is true, her life being backgrounded by the circumstances quoted from Dr. Richmond above.

During my entire working career I was identified with typical masculine occupations and activities. I was neither effeminate, nor personally permitted a hint of the inner femininity, which was a major part of my inner self and yet, for reasons which eluded my full understanding, I was seldom completely comfortable with my seeming outer masculinity. I carried on a war of resistance to my transsexual condition whenever necessary, but it was far from easy as also present in my mind was the fact that I was, it seemed, constantly in danger of being undermined by other circumstances in my life which fed my anxiety and stress.

Keep in mind that effeminacy and femininity are two differing influences even if related. Effeminacy is an outer manifestation linked to the inner feminine core of a man. It is often contrived and even exaggerated in an unnatural way. The effeminate man, who in any event is usually gay, sends out visible signals of his effeminacy. Typically these might include a mincing gait, limp wrists and a lisping manner of speech. There may also be a distinct preference for exaggerated female stylization, all of which invites the epithets of fag, sissy, and others. The effeminate man usually cannot help himself except in terms of perhaps going to greater excesses in clothing and life style.

Quite distinct from the effeminate man is the heterosexual man with a distinct but invariably well-hidden feminine core. This type can feel his femininity under his masculine exterior and the two can be in severe internal conflict. The outer shell works very hard to contain the inner core and is invariably fearful that he will ever let his guard down and shamefully expose this inner self, the inner woman of transsexual folklore. Externally he is ashamed of her inner influence but internally, as a palliative to his bouts of stress, anxiety and depression caused essentially by these two differing and not necessarily conflicting personalities, he derives hidden satisfaction from her presence. She exists in his mind and maybe even carries the image of a woman whom he idolizes. Often he resents her as hidden baggage of some sort, occasionally he may hate her for her unwelcome intrusions, but more often in a strange way he likes her and may even at times fall in love with the image in his mind.

I offer this interpretation of a typical heterosexual transsexual, that is heterosexual at least in his origins, who in many instances resents any suggestion that men are attractive to him, because they are not. Often he feels more at home with women, and as in my own case, finds it easy and appealing to form friendships with women and, as in my past, equally easy to fall in love with them. It might be associated with a gallant view of a woman as the recipient of this respect and even love, which she does not always deserve. My two marriages started in each instance as infatuations which became romantic affairs where common-sense caution was overtaken by a vision of perfection. While it is not unique to heterosexual transsexuals, I will, to this day as a new woman, readily form friendships with women, and although they are not romantic in any lesbian sense, I will give them my loyalty and respect and will make a real effort to accommodate myself to a wholly compatible friendship, where kindly sensitive gestures and considerations each way are of great importance to me. I might add that this applies equally to the handful of sex-changed women who are, like myself, former transsexuals, whom I count as friends. I could add the caveat that if such friendships ever developed on a romantic or sexual level, then they would be classified as lesbian. Obviously, this can and does develop with some so that the orientation of a person following gender reassignment surgery is more of a consideration than their former orientation prior to surgery.

In my experience of this scene I have met a score or more of heterosexual formerly male transsexuals with similar experiences and outlooks. Often they have been professionals in some field such as engineering or flying. Occasionally like myself they have come from a business background, and in all instances they have sought happiness after sometimes going through some of the most extraordinary personal experiences imaginable.

Two come to mind, one was a bush pilot and the other a field biologist and both were highly secretive crossdressers. Their excursions into the remote wilderness gave them their only outlets in terms of allowing the woman inside to have free rein out in the wilderness. Eventually this form of subterfuge got to them. It felt less than honest, it was artificially constricted by their circumstances, and the knowledge that things could have been far different if nature had taken a different turn caused both to eventually face the music and get their lives onto a better and more open basis. Today both have gone through the entire course of gender reassignment and are happy women with good prospects for the future.

Don't ever try to tell me that transsexualism is a product of insanity alone, or some errant form of an imagination running riot. When you have lived almost all your life with an awareness of its presence and, as in my case and many others, have been aware of it since as early as age three, long before there was any appreciation of human sexuality, you are not likely to accept any suggestion from anyone that it is all in your mind and that given time "you will grow out of it." Quite the contrary, in fact, it is fully recognised by those who understand and specialize in the treatment of the condition that it does develop *in utero* and is a lifetime condition which never leaves the subject and is only likely to intensify with age. Happily its effects can be neutralized under a course of treatment already alluded to.

To overlook the biological origins of the condition is like being told on every occasion that you are a "bloody liar, a charlatan," and yet this is what Kathy Johnson suffered for many years at the hands of one prison official after another. In fact, many of these people are so intransigent in their view of things that only a bulldozer or a cabinet minister seem to have sufficient strength or power to shift them off their perches. They are civil servants and too often with civil servants there is an attitude of preserving their own onion patches at the expense of the very people they are supposed to be serving. In the case of a prison official the attitude too often is that he is protecting the public and that the criminal wrongdoer must pay for his crimes and hang the cost in terms of taxpayer's money.

Maybe I am coming through to some readers as a bleeding heart liberal. In truth all my instincts are usually conservative. I do see the merit of the death penalty as a means of ridding society of the worst sorts of murderers like the serial and the cold calculating premeditated killers who are all too common today and simply become an expensive burden on an already overburdened system. I do see the merit of physical punishment[10] as being a means to contain and manage trends in a child which if allowed to run rampant can lead to all sorts of excesses. In short, if you break the law and perpetrate harm to another person or property you do and must expect to pay the price, it's as simple as that. But in whatever form, justice must be tempered with moderation and a true effort to make the punishment fit the crime.

To make a child kneel on hard grains of rice on a kitchen floor for periods of time because of failure to tie his shoelaces properly, and for the failure of the father to intervene, is as cruel and callous as the very act of punishment which was devised by Kathy's stepmother. Today that woman, who is still alive, has much to answer for, not just for the intemperate way in which she behaved, but also because irreparable harm was done to a child who had no defence or recourse. It was the very act of cruel and unusual punishment which was the precursor to a life of crime and waste.

Dr. Guy Richmond probably had vastly more expertise as a prison doctor than most, and he gained his experience in

---

[10] The recent punishment of an American youth in Singapore, who was flogged according to Singaporean law for wanton vandalism, is a process from which western lawmakers could learn in dealing with similar problems in our own society.

Britain's infamous Dartmoor Prison before moving to a similar position in Canada at the Oakalla Institution in Burnaby, B.C. Again we quote from his book *Prison Doctor,* Chapter Thirteen entitled "Prisoners Are Also People":

> *On the whole there has been little change in the punitive basis of prisons as opposed to some training establishments such as young offenders' units, camps and open prisons. It is in the more secure and traditionally administered prisons that we meet those with the greatest need for all the understanding, skilful and compassionate guidance which can be offered by people who respect the inherent dignity of man. Psychiatrists are constantly faced with the firmly established tradition that treatment is treatment and custody is custody and never the twain shall meet.*
>
> *One of the main conflicts between treatment and custody is between rigid gaol (jail) rules which were intended to control prisoners, and therapeutic techniques of trying to disperse hostility by education towards self-imposed controls and by group participation to develop member's awareness. There are two opposite reactions when a prison officer is told to go and fuck himself and when a therapist is told to go and do the same. The prison officer usually feels compelled to take action and that action is exactly what the offender expected and perhaps intended to evoke, namely the laying of a charge which almost certainly ends in punishment. It's the same old rat race— hostility, rebellion, counteraction by authority, feelings of self-pity, resentment and anger; or indifference and resignation. The barrier is reinforced. The therapist, on the other hand, invites the prisoner to throw off his*

cloak of hatred and see what he looks like without it. The therapist knows that someone who is conditioned to respond to prison authority with the usual antagonism will be at a loss if he can draw no heat; then, when his defences are down, he is most likely to be receptive to counselling by a therapist with whom he has a good relationship.

Dr. Richmond's comments effectively define the barrier which exists between the prison system and its outside therapists. The most comprehensive assessment was that undertaken in the Watson/Diewold report, but realistically the two consultants might have saved their time for all the impact their report had on the prison hierarchy. When one considers some of the internal reports from one management level to another in Corrections it can readily be seen that many of the problems for inmates such as Kathy were fully generated by the system itself.

For an example let us take a look at memorandum 23231 dated July 6, 1981, prepared by Parole Service Officer Richard A. Scovil, conducted at the Regional Psychiatric Centre for Ontario. This report followed a meeting when Kathy's application for parole by exception was considered. We quote:

A Case Conference was held with Dr. William Maley, Clinical Director, R.P.C. (Ontario), Rose Morelli, Psychologist, R.P.C. (Ontario), and the undersigned. Immediately following the Case Conference an individual interview was conducted with the SUBJECT.

JOHNSON'S application by exception states that he is making application as "Further incarceration is putting my medical and mental health in jeopardy. . . ." This statement was discussed with JOHNSON as were the other statements on his parole application. JOHNSON claims that he is liable to end his own life as a result of his not receiving proper treatments for transsexuality (sic). It was indicated to him that he is to be provided with reasonable medical health care and that treatment for transsexuality may not fall within the definition of reasonable. He claims that he has taken female hormones, however, these were taken illegally and had not been prescribed for him. With respect to JOHNSON's suicidal statements it was pointed out to him that his unstable conduct in the institutions, to wit, suicide and self-mutilation is not new.

This man is now in his early thirties and it is only since 1976 that he himself has been stating he is transsexual. Recent research in this area (a Swedish study) indicate that the criteria for success (i.e. satisfied clients), are - the age at which the client indicates feminine traits (5 to 6 years old) - no prior drug involvement - no heterosexual contact - no criminal activity. It can be seen that JOHNSON does not meet any of these criteria. His drug addiction and homosexuality and other indications of anti-social behaviour date to his early teens (14 years).

During the Case Conference with Dr. Maley it was indicated that JOHNSON's mental and physical health are not considered at risk as JOHNSON would be as disturbed now if he were not claiming to be a transsexual as he is at the present time. It was further indicated in the Case Conference that we are still waiting to hear from Dr. Craigen, but that we could not expect a recommendation or policy from Ottawa that surgery be employed. The only possibility would be that *hormones and counselling could be employed, but as yet we have no policy.*

I enclose a memo from the Medical Director, Regional Psychiatric Centre (Ontario) dated 3rd of June, 1981, a package of information from the Medical Records Department, Regional Psychiatric Centre (Pacific) and a package from the Vancouver General Hospital. The information in these reports is self-evident.

On the basis of the information received to date, and my discussion with Dr. Maley, Rose Morelli, and the SUBJECT I have no choice at the present time other than to recommend Parole Denied by Exception."

First let us deal with the other two participants. Rose Morelli can hardly have made up her mind about the prisoner on the basis of one interview. In fact, her report of 1986 (quoted in the previous chapter) which was the result of a whole succession of interviews of Kathy Johnson over a period of some six years takes a considerably different tack to that implied by Scovil in the foregoing. As for Dr. Maley, Kathy recalls that he was an old man probably not far from retirement who had been consistently negative towards her. Whether this was entirely personal or simply because she is transsexual, she is uncertain, but on the balance of probabilities it was more than likely because of the latter. Apart from that the one statement attributed to him is a matter of belief with no evidence presented which would make it into a matter of fact.

Scovil's report ignores an important aspect of Kathy's previous case history. That concerns two of many acts (1) the suicide attempt when she very nearly succeeded in taking her own life by cutting her jugular vein and (2) her successful self-castration. To cut the jugular seems to be the act of a person under the most severe duress, where death seems a better option than life itself. One also wonders why self-castration would be undergone by a man who valued his masculinity and had every intention of remaining a man. We have asked the question before, but it bears repeating. Do not these two single acts indicate an individual in the greatest distress and why would Scovil largely brush it aside in his report? It is true, Scovil does say he pointed out "that his unstable conduct in the institutions, to wit, suicide and self-mutilation, is not new." So what? Does one have to be bringing up new circumstances all the time when dealing with a lifetime problem. The sheer consistency of Kathy's tack on the subject was more indicative of her state of mind than anything else.

Instead we read what was probably the professional judgement of Dr. Maley that "Johnson's mental and physical health are not considered to be at risk as Johnson would be as disturbed now as if he were not claiming to be a transsexual." As has just been noted self-castration hardly seems to be the choice of a man who is not transsexual.

Scovil is scornful when he makes mention of the fact that Kathy had only been stating her conviction of her transsexualism since 1976. The implication is clear that Scovil suggests that Kathy had stumbled on this situation within herself like a child finding a new toy. She was actually 29 at the time and it can only be added that it is quite typical for a self-admission of transsexualism to come out many years after the first self-awareness becomes apparent within the subject. I received my first message from nature stating that there was something different in my sexuality in that I found an inner femininity at the age of three and a half years. I did not succeed in properly defining it until I was 19 and I did not mention it to a living soul until reaching the age of 62! This secrecy and self-repression is one of the tragedies of transsexualism and it arises largely because of the stereotypical straightjacket which is forced on to anyone who is even a little different.

Scovil makes mention of a Swedish study. Maybe he believed it to be reliable in 1981, but understanding then and subsequent knowledge refutes this. The client does not have to indicate feminine traits at 5 to 6 years old. If such exists it is usually entirely in the mind and remains a carefully guarded secret until it finally comes out commonly under severe duress at almost any age. He adds "no prior drug involvement, no heterosexual contact, no criminal activity" as being further indicators. These are irrelevant factors in determining the incidence of transsexualism. Lots of transsexuals have had an involvement with drugs and some with criminal activities probably in about the same ratio as the general population.

What he means by "no heterosexual contact" is nothing short of bizarre. What I think he meant was that to be transsexual one had to be homosexual. Almost the opposite in fact is true as the record shows that a probable majority of all transsexuals come from basic heterosexual backgrounds. He clearly does not appreciate the difference between the transsexual and the sexual orientation of homosexuality.

A final comment on this report. The taking of hormones is not illegal. It is not an indictable offence. He must have confused hormones with illegal drugs like heroin. When taken under proper supervision hormones are available by prescription. When purchased through the street black-market it is certainly highly likely that self-prescription is most unwise, particularly as many transsexual buyers tend to overdose. But under what act or statute they become illegal is not known or identifiable because no such law exists. I suppose if you use the word illegal often enough in a supposed expert report others reading it will come to accept it, which adds further to the bad name of the subject person.

A further report originated with Richard Scovil dated November 5, 1981. In this Confidential Information Report (C.I.R.) the following statements are set out:

> *The purpose of this C.I.R. is to draw attention to the previous C.I.R. on file and to indicate the institutional viewpoint. JOHNSON is viewed variously as untrustworthy, dangerous, self-seeking, egocentric etc.*
>
> *JOHNSON's previous behaviour has been blamed upon heroin addiction and now JOHNSON is blaming the heroin addiction on his transsexuality. JOHNSON is also blaming everything else that happened in his life on transsexuality and it seems to the undersigned that this is a convenient hook on which to hang life's problems. Undoubtedly a true transsexual, should such a thing exist, would be able to relate most of life's difficulties to his condition and it may be that Johnson truly believes what he says. It does seem however, that JOHNSON has compartmentalized his life to the point where one single thing is the cause of all troubles.*

There is no indication that Kathy does now, or ever did, blame all her troubles on her transsexualism. Given her background and record it seems reasonable to suppose that her committal to a criminal life would have been far more absolute. It may sound strange to say it, given everything else which has been explained in this book, but it is probable that her transsexual nature gave rise to a far more peaceable personality than otherwise might have been the case. If one is transsexual the condition simply has to be lived with just as the colour of one's eyes or the shape of the skull are with you for life. I have never heard a transsexual blame all his/her problems on the condition. Transsexuals have never been heard to say that they are glad they are transsexual. Is anyone ever glad that they were born with any handicap? They only say they are glad they have dealt with their condition once they have it behind them. At least they have a better chance of leading a more tranquil life.

Noteworthy also is mention in the first report quoted above that among the documents forwarded with the report is a package from Vancouver General Hospital with the comment that the information in these reports is self-evident. Indeed, that information was self-evident because it was the Watson/Diewold report which we set out in full in the previous chapter. If that report is referred to again it will be seen that Dr. Watson gave the warning that if some steps are not taken toward gender reassignment "Douglas (Kathy) will prove a most difficult management problem in prison and will most likely be a risk for suicide and self-mutilation."

At this point it is necessary to put the clock back to October 20, 1980. Ms. Clare Culhaine, the prisoners' rights advocate, had raised the issue of Kathy's hormone treatment. She was arrogantly replied to by Dr. Stanley Webb and this exchange of correspondence was quoted in the previous chapter. Ms. Culhaine requested an opinion from Dr. Watson and asked her to respond to Dr. Webb's letter. We quote:

Dear Dr. Webb,

Re: Douglas (Kathy) Johnson
Inmate #5526

I have just received a letter from Ms. Claire Culhaine of the Prisoner's Rights Group requesting my opinion and a response to your letter of September 9, 1980, addressed to her regarding the above-named.

I am a fully qualified psychiatrist licensed to practice in the Province of B.C. and I have, in addition, spent two years training with the Sexual Medicine Unit of the Vancouver General Hospital, where my special interest was in the area of gender disorders. As you may or may not be aware, Douglas, who prefers to be called Kathy, was referred to me for assessment by Dr. Saad of the Regional Psychiatric Centre in Abbotsford, B.C., and an extensive evaluation was performed in May and June, 1980. The evaluation process included a complete psychiatric interview, psychological testing (performed by Pat Diewold, a psychologist who works with the Sexual Medicine Unit and has considerable expertise and experience in evaluating gender dysphoria) and physical and laboratory investigations. I enclose a copy of my report which summarises my observations and recommendations. If you require more specific information with regard to any aspect of this report I will gladly forward it on request.

Please note that on page 4 of my report I recommend that "Douglas be given a trial on hormones and be requested to dress and function to the greatest extent possible in the female role." I go on to say that "I feel there is a possibility of rehabilitation in the female role as Douglas has many positive attributes. . . ." I do not feel that Douglas is likely to adjust as a male, even if the self-inflicted castration was not taken into consideration. "If some steps are not taken toward sex reassignment Douglas will prove to be a most difficult management problem in prison and will most likely be a risk for suicide and self mutilation."

*I suggested that hormone administration should be
in the form of Diethylstilbestrol starting with 5-10 mg
daily, increasing to 15-20 mg daily if there are no signs
of intolerance.*

*In your letter (to Ms. Culhaine) you state
categorically that administration of female hormones is
inappropriate, unjustified and based on the demands of
the inmate. You state that this opinion is the consensus
of a number of physicians, but you do not indicate
whether consultation with specialists in the area of
gender dysphoria had any influence in your decision. In
July, 1980, I did forward a copy of my report to you in
care of Box 880, Kingston, Ontario. Am I to assume
that you did not receive it?*

Yours truly,

*D.B. Watson, M.D., F.R.C.P. (C)
Psychiatry*

There is much that is cynical in the handling of this case
by Webb and Scovil. It almost has the makings of a plot for one
of those episodes in the television serial *The Prisoner* featuring
actor Patrick McGoohan. Any hope McGoohan had of escaping
from the incarceration maze in which he found himself was
frustrated by hidden, faceless guards who addressed him without
being seen and without him being able to effectively reply.

Webb, it will be recalled, was the doctor who had earlier
offered Kathy testosterone medication following the self-
castration episode. It is virtually certain that his consultation with
other physicians was with his own type in the system and not, as
Dr. Watson clearly suspected, with specialists in the field of
gender dysphoria.

Scovil is open to criticism. He was clearly out of his depth and instead of displaying any sort of understanding he resorted to insults and innuendoes. He had no business in setting out what were clearly his own highly coloured and ignorant impressions. He cast doubt without basis on the condition of transsexualism "if such a thing exists." By what right did he set himself up above recognised specialists?

The one question therefore remains: Why do the prison authorities go through these rituals in protecting their autocracy? Who and what are they trying to appease? Not their own consciences as there is sometimes little evidence that such actually exist. Not public opinion, as the public seldom has much knowledge about the details of life behind prison walls. And as for the politicians, they seem to be blind-sided as much as anything by the bureaucracy which thrives regardless of the political party in power. The answer to that one eludes me; maybe someone else can provide it.

* * * * *

Prisoner of Gender

Chapter Fifteen

SOME CONCLUSIONS AND COMMENTS

The aspect of the prison system administration which is most noteworthy is the rigid, inflexible and ostrich-like attitude which is all too prevalent. It can hardly be said by its appearance to be doctrinaire. One gains the impression that it is more a matter of "That is the way we have always done it" or "What was good enough for the previous generation is good enough for me."

However, to that I would add that there are additional elements which go beyond the system's ultra-conservative mould to something infinitely more frightening. Those elements include supreme deceit and viciousness. In the previous chapter we set out reports from prison parole officer, R.B. Scovil. His handling, his statements and his conclusions and recommendations go against every psychiatric or psychological report rendered between the Watson/Diewold report of 1980 and the final assessment report rendered by Dr. Carl Bartashunas on January 25, 1991, in support of Kathy's parole application. Bartashunas was an outside consultant in private practice retained by the system for the purpose of assessing Kathy. There were also other reports in between including the Cormier letter and that of Rose Morelli, professionals employed within the prison system.

These reports differed in detail and some were necessarily brief and ringed by caveats, as being professional people they had to always maintain a responsible informed stance in keeping with the standards of their profession. But they all reached the same conclusion which was that Kathy Johnson was transsexual and that she would benefit by appropriate treatment.

To repeat the Bartashunas assessment of seven pages would be tedious for the reader as much that it contains has already been covered—different phraseology but the same meaning. Based on her past record it was not entirely favourable to Kathy. However it did note:

> *She (Kathy) did impress as being strongly feminine in outlook as well as tendencies and feelings and thus is highly likely a transsexual in the real sense of the word.*

The report concluded that:

> *Ms. Johnson should be seriously considered for parole given her current gender identity difficulties and partially completed sexual reassignment* (hormone therapy and self-castration—author's note), *she is misplaced in her incarceration in a male institution and further incarceration at this point would probably not be of benefit to her.*

What is also very worrying is the attitude that "we have no policy" (and unless someone kicks them into action they never will). What this indicates is a lack of forward thinking, a failure to keep up with the times, and perhaps a belief that these publicly paid administrators do not want to be disturbed in their comfortable pew. The attitude is not confined to the prison system. It is common in our churches and in other branches of government.

I admit that I only have recent knowledge gained from working on Kathy's story, doing research and most importantly, examining the file of supportive documents in depth. Like many others in the large unaffected outside population I was astounded with much that I came across. I simply had no idea as to what went on behind prison walls other than what occasionally came out in the daily newspapers or television news items, or the creations of Hollywood. I was even naive enough to accept that prisoners are handled with humanity and compassion as befits the Canadian tradition. After all, are we not the world's great peacekeepers extolling our role as unexcitable humanitarian non-colonialists, non-imperialists and a host of other good things? For me stumbling into the truth of the situation through official documents was rather like falling into a sewer.

Long-term imprisonment is mind-boggling in its potential for changing the characteristics of prisoners. It is unnatural to shut a person away for many years on end and yet society has not devised and seems unlikely to ever devise a better system. It is not just a matter of inflicting punishment, it also becomes a matter of public security and the liberalization of many of our official attitudes to the application of the law and imprisonment, all of which bring on severe reactionary pressure for greater punishment as the pendulum swings back to the other more conscrvative extreme. Much is made of the cost of imprisonment and we have done this to some extent ourselves in this narrative, but just as much or more can be made of the cost of keeping a wrongdoer out of prison. Society is caught on the horns of a dilemma torn between attitudes of "lock 'em up and throw away the key" and the opposite which supports an ever softer approach towards liberalization when prisons will no longer be necessary. There is no easy answer.

What working on Kathy's story has forcefully brought home to me is the need for improved and even new attitudes for dealing with street crime and all the evils it brings. Drugs are probably the most central issue, as from drug abuse grows the need to support the habit through thieving, robbery, prostitution and far worse. Recent publicity on the part of newspaper reports and television news features brings home the fact that on Vancouver's streets alone there may now be a few thousand of actual or potential Kathys (even if not transsexual), where they ran to hundreds at most in her day. Also in her day we did not have the disease of AIDS. Most of these street kids will end up in trouble with the law or contaminated by HIV or both. Stealing, breaking and entering, and bank robbery are all too prevalent in Canadian cities and Vancouver can only be regarded as one of the worst affected.

Why do kids find their way into the crime spots? Most frequently it starts at home with sexual, physical or even psychological abuse, parents who don't care, set a bad example, fail to communicate or abrogate their responsibilities and a host of other negative influences. The gang and drug culture pervades our high schools and the process of recruitment starts at an early age. The kids are lured to the bright lights and supposed glamour of the brightly lit street, but behind this facade is a jungle of back lanes, decaying flophouses, and human predators like pimps and drug pushers only too keen to turn potentially good kids into trash to suit their own purposes. Once caught in the viciousness of this scene they invariably become lost souls and follow routes that are all too familiar; dead on a park bench or in a public toilet overdosed or wracked by alcohol, or if they survive, in jail for terms which expose them even further to all the extremes of a prison environment.

We cannot always blame parents. I have personally known responsible loving parents who have brought a child into this world who is so profoundly disturbed as to be unmanageable. About a year ago Vancouverites were astounded by media interviews of a fine-looking ten-year old boy. His mother and stepfather were at their wits ends in trying to control the boy who even then was a veteran car thief and obviously very street smart. The family home was located in a reasonably average area. When interviewed the boy revealed no shame and was smug about the fact that the law could do nothing with him until he reached the age of 12. That boy is a perfect candidate for a pre-ordained life of imprisonment and unless some spark of change for the better gets into him very soon that is the way he will surely go.

Only yesterday evening I watched a segment on a television news program concerning a Vancouver mother who has tried to bring up her daughter with solid worthwhile values. The girl found her way into prostitution and it was only with much effort that she managed to get the girl off the street and bring her home. It worked for a short while and then the girl slipped away again, but now the mother recognises that despite her best efforts the girl has a demon in her and cannot be held. Now the mother's attitude is that the next move must be her daughter's, that is to return because she wants to. She also recognises that that may never happen and her daughter may be lost forever.

Why children from good middle-class homes succumb is always a good question. Again drug exposure is a common problem, but also there can be anger at some supposed or real deprivation, the lure of a boyfriend or unsavoury friends, early childhood abuse and the overall pressures and demoralization in society by which parents themselves can be placed in a bad position, unable for work pressure or economic reasons to provide adequate supervision, leadership or the good example so necessary in any family environment.

One can say "There, but for the grace of God, go I" and there is much truth in this. My own son and daughter have successfully traversed this valley of extreme danger which sometimes engulfs people who have come from so-called better class homes and families. I do know that both experimented like many others while in high school and were subject to influences which could have ruined their lives had they taken the wrong turn, but whatever the shortcomings existing in their parents' relationship, the fact that they had solid home values to lean on greatly reduced the danger. Equally it has to be recognized that it was also a different society then.

A young woman friend told me recently of her own experience and the need for a strong family background. Evidently her mother was not only schizoid, but was heavily dependent on alcohol. The father could not handle this so he deserted the family and started a new one. She described her brother and herself as being extremely poor through childhood. She found solace in alcohol and cocaine as soon as she had any money of her own. The night she was first going to shoot up with a speed ball along with her boyfriend was the night that she decided that she had to turn her life around. Whether she saw some sort of light she is uncertain, but the knowledge of what a speed ball is and can do gave her sufficient of a fright to recognize that she was at a critical turn in her life.

The boyfriend took the drug and passed out. She held back, managed to give up cocaine and drugs generally. She joined Alcoholics Anonymous and over the past ten years has been free of alcohol and drugs holding down a very good job with excellent prospects for the future. She has a pleasing outgoing personality ideally suited to her job. She can afford an expensive sports car and holidays away. In other words she is in a position to fully benefit from her labours, but that one moment of decision likely changed her life forever. Equally likely she avoided a life of degradation, prostitution and crime. What her story does show is that there is a knife edge along which all of us travel, and it is so easy to come down on the wrong side.

Drugs are the most pernicious and destructive of all the adverse influences which affect society. Estimates vary as to the percentage of all crime which has its origins in drugs, but a frequent one is around 80 per cent. Why then cannot society do something to reduce this destructive influence? Well, it seems we are incapable of accommodating ourselves to the idea that drug distribution for profit is the most probable answer. It is simply too attractive for crime starting with the cocaine cartels of Medallin and Calli in Columbia, and the heroin industries of Burma, Thailand and Pakistan. The only answer we seem to have in North America is interdiction and no doubt that is very important, but Kathy's story tells me clearly that if the profit is taken out of drug pushing on the street and in the jails themselves we would be taking an even bigger step in reducing crime.

Kathy is the first one to admit the extent of her crimes. In spite of the devastating and ugly remarks of officialdom in the previous chapter, I have in fact been deeply touched by the candour and honesty which she has shown all along since we started working on this project. Once hooked on heroin she became enslaved in the manner of all drug addicts and because of this her prison history was greatly extended.

Other than alcohol, comparatively few in my generation have been tempted by drugs. We escaped much of that and the idea for me of ever taking any habit-forming drug has never had any appeal under any circumstances. On the other hand I remember my consternation when I was phoned by the police and advised that my then 16-year old daughter had been arrested following a minor drug bust when they found her and a group of her teenage high school friends in a local restaurant after they had been visited by a hash and marijuana distributor whom the police were watching.

When I went to the local police station to reclaim my errant daughter I was confronted by a thoroughly frightened and weeping teenager. I think she was the last one of the group to be called for by a parent and I think the experience had a salutary effect on her and quite a profound effect on me. If nothing else it brought home to me that my responsibility as a parent was an ongoing thing which would not go out like switching off an electric light. Today that daughter is 37 years old and is a thoroughly responsible young woman over whom I still have natural concerns, but they are those of the surviving parent whose main interest is to see her children well set on their courses through life for long after I have left these shores.

Not too long after my book *Feelings* came out I was asked some questions by a friend who is in his forties. He had worked with me in the production of the book. He is the father of a son and younger daughter and my book had caused him to think. He asked me one day quite out of the blue how he should handle a factor that could appear in either of his children which might indicate some influence such as gender dysphoria.

I told him what would be my advice to anyone with a difficulty to deal and live with. Communicate, communicate, communicate. Add to this patience and the ability to listen. Communication is not a one-way street. Too often the parent feels he/she is communicating through reading the Riot Act. Delivering an ultimatum is hardly communication on a level playing field, but sometimes when all else has run out it is the only remaining course of action. All the foregoing are extremely important in all relationships, but none more so than in that between a parent and child. The attitude that even the slightest hint of an aberration can be beaten out like stamping out a grass fire is totally erroneous. It is far better to get it out in the open, if possible, where it then has a chance of receiving decent attention and understanding with always a good chance that the worst effects can be headed off or at least reduced.

How I would have liked to talk over my own problems as a child with an understanding parent. My late mother, bless her, whom I loved greatly, seemed to be in perpetual confrontation with my father who dominated the family to the exclusion of all else. My father could only be engaged in any conversation on his terms. He was always too ready for confrontation and too lacking in the ability to understand anyone else's point of view and as a child I lived in fear of him. When I did eventually learn to be honest with myself as my life related to my condition of gender dysphoria, I found to my great advantage that it also loosened my tongue in such a way that I could be totally open and honest with others in explaining my problems. In fact, it added a new dimension and quality to my life. From being sometimes a morose, tight-lipped, rather reserved individual I suddenly found myself able to give of myself and even smile where I had found this impossible before.

Contrast this to the position of Kathy over most of her life. A difficult, near impossible home life, out of the school system at grade three, on the street, into a reform school at 10 and graduating to hard drugs by 14. This is tough stuff in anyone's language. There was no one more educated she would come into contact with than a school teacher and in most instances she was simply written off as out of control. Admittedly she did improve her education to grade eleven while in the system, but beyond that her sole society was the prison crowd and even when free on the street it was nearly impossible to avoid them as they often tended to gravitate to certain specific spots such as the intersection of Main and East Hastings in Vancouver.

She was bound by the prison code, one simply does not rat on a fellow prisoner. Twice at least she could have avoided imprisonment for up to three years if the truth had come out. The most noteworthy was the hold-up of a corner store while she was being driven to her halfway house at Hamilton. The wrongdoer thought he could bluff his way out in some way by pleading "not guilty," and just as she was bound by her interpretation of the code, the wrongdoer evidently never spared a thought about implicating Kathy. This part of the savagery of prison life, who cares about self-elevation and who gives a damn about pulling others down with them, just boggles the mind of the outsider!

What are the possibilities of reform in such a way that incarcerated transsexual people could derive some hope for a better future? They serve time for what they did, not for what they are. But because they are what they are, is it necessary to add torture, depravity and sexual mayhem to the list of punishments they have to endure?

To summarise much that we have discussed, one has to ask:

1. Why engage experts to render educated informed diagnoses if they are simply filed "no action" or follow the prisoner around like a mutant paper trail, without force or effect?

2. Is there no sensible financial mind in the entire system that is capable of adding up the financial cost, because anyone with an ounce of intelligence and an ability to do simple arithmetic can see in this day of budget constraints that money is simply wastefully poured down a deep hole by the system? Treatment would have cost so little, stupidity and neglect have cost so much.

3. Where is our sense of compassion and ordinary decent humanity? Would we allow dogs to be exposed to these inhuman constraints? Again the logical mind has to wonder why it should be considered so impossible that a small specialised facility could not be developed within one of our prisons. There are, at most, maybe a dozen or two affected people in the prison system at any one time. Put them together, let them live their lifestyle within reason, within the prison walls, but above all at moderate cost and let them have the benefit of some specialised care which would modify the extremities of their behaviour patterns, which are probably made extreme by the evils of the system. A refusal and failure to develop some reasonable parameters have cost Kathy a great deal in terms of her present and future health and a probable reduced life expectancy.

4. Constantly the system has let bigotry, ignorance and pure prejudice rule the day. Penology is taught as a university course and doctorates are awarded within the discipline, but it is near certain that if the subject of transsexuals within the prison system receives any attention it will be more concerned with how to warehouse them and less concerned with bringing about a happier and more effective conclusion where they can emerge more fulfilled as human beings after serving their sentences.

5. There is a need for a legal definition of transsexualism which would be an extension on the medical definition. This would not be to create a new class of citizen, but should give some reasonable protection to the transsexual when the individual's life is most fraught with peril and nowhere would this be more valuable than in the prison system. This is a human right issue for all transsexuals and a health issue for most of us where we want to live our lives as normally, enjoyably, productively and creatively as we can.

6. Rules of conduct can be developed for the handling of transsexual cases. The subject goes through a private hell, but with consideration and knowledge his/her course can be made far easier without exposing him to the incredible dangers he now faces. As an example take the federal and B.C. provincial guidelines set out in Appendix II and compare the two. The provincial rules, while not perfect, are far ahead of the federal.

7. All along we find references in medical assessment and prison reports which try to suggest that Kathy was not under mental stress and did not need treatment. We find others who refuse to give treatment in the face of affirmative specialist reports. One wonders how they viewed Kathy's history of suicide attempts, was it merely a matter of drawing attention to herself as one report suggests. To castrate oneself and seek to cut off the penis strikes this writer as going beyond any normal extreme, even though these acts were not of themselves suicide attempts. Worse still a deep cut to the jugular hardly suggests some light-hearted exhibitionism. Did it not occur to these judgement-makers that she really did want to end her life given her extreme misery?

The fact that she survived within the system was a matter of good or bad luck depending on how one might make a judgement, but nonetheless it also indicates a degree of intestinal fortitude quite beyond that which would ever have been displayed by some of her big tough-guy male acquaintances. They would have long since departed from this world, broken men. Was the dullard prison management system so slow on the uptake that it could just never occur to them that Kathy meant what she said when she spoke of her gender dysphoria and that life was simply not worth living unless she had some hope of a new life in accord with her feminine being?

* * * * *

Working with Kathy Johnson has, in spite of the misery and the endless traumatic events in her life, been a real pleasure. It has brought a new friendship to each of our lives and we are both the richer for the experience. However, it has not been without its moments of pain for Kathy who has had to relive experiences which were slowly fading from her consciousness.

For myself there have been nightmare moments as I have lain in bed thinking over a discussion and then playing it out afresh as if I was an actor in a drama. There were lots of self-addressed questions as to how I would have handled a given circumstance. There was also a realization of the quagmire in which Kathy found herself over much of her life. Sometimes I would become so upset about the horrors of imprisonment, particularly the type of dangerous, near hopeless imprisonment one reads of now and again. These would bring to mind pictures of a child caught in one of those horrible impasses such as being trapped down a well shaft, or coal miners entrapped deep down in a coal mine following an explosion. In those nightmare circumstances there was no sleep for me as I lay in my comfortable bed.

I have no doubt there will be scornful comments about this book when certain people read it. There will be ridicule with remarks like "She only got what she deserved, serves her right for being a transsexual" and similar. I only ask that the reader keep his or her sense of proportion. Imprisonment for crimes committed is one thing and that has never been minimized in this account. But she was not imprisoned for being transsexual as transsexualism is neither a crime nor a civil offence.

In very large measure much of Kathy's suffering was attributable to the punishing attitude of the prison system which if nothing else encouraged a torture regime for transsexuals by its own acts of conscious omission. Even today Corrections Canada and the National Parole Board are coming under more or less continuous criticism in such a way that there are clearly mounting demands for reform and revision. Regrettably there is little evidence that in the minds of most critics these demands also encompass the needs of transsexual prisoners. I believe this book brings out a clear case for considerable rethinking of policy in handling transsexuals and this much should be taken into account in any move to improve conditions for such people. For once it would be gratifying to see transsexuals dealt with as a positive, definable and understood minority rather than see them falling by the wayside like so much garbage dropping off the truck.

By her own definition Kathy has grown a lot as the result of the effort put out in writing this book. As she said herself, this has given her an objective and a reason for living beyond the ordinary routines of routine days. For Kathy this experience has broadened her horizon. There is a better appreciation that there is life beyond tomorrow and that all the tomorrows can be extended into the promise of weeks, months and years of enjoyable life.

* * * * *

We have discussed much in Kathy's past. What of Kathy's future now that she has told her story? She feels that it is a lot brighter and I am very much inclined to agree with her. She has achieved something she never thought possible and that alone is a great boost to self-confidence. She has natural talents which have seldom had adequate scope for expression. So how can she make a contribution to society?

She sees a possible role as a counsellor using her own extensive hands-on experience, particularly in dealing with the younger generation. She recalls that she was something of a mother figure while in male institutions, younger inmates often visiting her, with a guard's permission, to seek her advice on all manner of subjects, including family matters which are invariably the greatest source of concern to prisoners. Few know better than her the travails and trauma of imprisonment and now in retrospect, how to avoid it by counting the cost before rather than after the wrongdoing.

She told me of an incident when she was doing volunteer kitchen work at a local fundamentalist church. She told the pastor one day of her transsexualism and her hopes for completing the process of gender change. Very soon after and without reason or warning she received a terse letter notifying her that her services were no longer required or her presence welcome.

It was a total put-down and carried with it the implication that this church's "perfect flock" might be in danger of becoming corrupted by the Kathy's of this world. The wisdom which should have been displayed, but was woefully lacking, was that the perfect flock could have learned from Kathy something of genuine value, including something of humanity and compassion.

One final point: transsexualism may seem complex and for many it probably is, but with a calm and sensible approach it is far from being impossible to understand. Remember it is a natural condition which in its worst form can be described as an illness, but it is not a disease and it is not a sexual orientation. Successful handling can bring great relief and a much improved personality.

On the very day that I am writing these words my anonymous friend who was mentioned by me in Chapter Eight was interviewed on a local radio station. She is now a recovering alcoholic and has given up drugs. She is now a far trimmer woman and with improved health and appearance she has good prospects ahead of her. In 1993 she had been challenged by her own doctor with the admonition that if she did not get her life under control and eliminate her alcohol and drug abuse, her future, sooner rather than later, was a one-way trip to the morgue. One can see readily enough that because she dealt with this problem and simultanously faced her transsexualism she now has a future. The radio interview on a well-known talk show brought her accolades which she richly deserved and her forthright honest approach can only help the cause of all transsexuals.

That is all that Kathy expects and hopes for in presenting her own forthright and honest story.

* * * * *

APPENDICES

THE WATSON TABLE
CATEGORIES OF GENDER DISORIENTATION AND INDECISION
MALE TO FEMALE

PROFILE	GROUP 1 Low Intensity Transvestite	GROUP 2 Moderate Intensity Transvestite	GROUP 3 Transvestitic Transsexual	GROUP 4 Moderate Intensity Transsexual	GROUP 5 High Intensity Transsexual
GENDER IDENTITY	Feminine identification only with acting out of sexual fantasies	Appeal for Feminity may spill over into non-sexual life	Ambivalent gender identity. Value male sex organs but feel feminine. "She-Male"	Feel female but able to suppress until age 30-50. Increasing dichotomy with age.	Total gender inversion. Never able to suppress femininity. Feminine boys.
GENDER ROLE	Normal male. Cross-dressing intermittent and private	Cross-dressing more pressured, fetishistic and exhibitionistic. Intermittent relapse of intense need to act on feminine impulses related to stress alternating with reduced desire.	Dresses as much as possible dependent on life circumstances. Dressing not necessarily sexual. Impulses often intensify with age and may crystalize later into a transsexual picture.	Try macho lifestyle to compensate. Increasing depression and anxiety over time. Never comfortable as males.	Dressing insufficient relief. Cross-live early.
EROTICISM	Genital-heightened arousal when cross-dressed.	Genital-some breast.	Genital and breast.	Genital if fantasizing self as female. Low libido.	Often asexual.
BIOLOGICAL FEMINIZATION	No desire.	If impulses ego-alien may use spironolactone to reduce libido.	Spironolactone for demasculinization + gynecomastia. Some may need hormones for emotional balance.	Requested late or intermittent.	Urgent request. Late teens, early 20's.

PROFILE	GROUP 1 Low Intensity Transvestite	GROUP 2 Moderate Intensity Transvestite	GROUP 3 Transvestitic Transsexual	GROUP 4 Moderate Intensity Transsexual	GROUP 5 High Intensity Transsexual
CONFLICTS	Guilt over normalcy, spousal disapproval.	Guilt and sexual performance anxiety, threatened masculinity fear of aging.	Confusion and personality disorganization, dual personality with male and female names and dissociated personality components.	Guilt, loss + fear of passing. Fear of rejection. Confused sexual orientation.	Stigma of re-assignment. Family and cultural attitudes.
DESIRE FOR RE-ASSIGNMENT	Not considered.	Fleeting under stress	May consider late if very inadequate as males, dependent on commitments.	Re-assignment hoped for, often attained.	Urgently requested. Self-mutilate if too long frustrated.
TREATMENT	Provide information and reassurance. Couples therapy. If impulses are ego-alien use behavior modification, setting limits on cross-dressing sufficient to control guilt but enough to allow emotional relief.	Insight-oriented psychotherapy to identify and modify sources of stress. Negotiate compromise in transvestitic behaviour such as dressing under male clothing.	Integrative psychotherapy to stabilize androgeny. Support for re-assignment if appropriate.	Supportive psycotherapy for symptomatic relief, family therapy. education group for stabilization of female identity.	Education support and family therapy. Assisting process of re-assignment.

223

Appendix II

Authority Conferred Within the Freedom of Information Act: Federal and Provincial Rules Dealing With Transsexuals in Prison

When the project to publish Kathy Johnson's story first evolved the publisher took the prudent step of checking with Corrections Canada on the matter of using or quoting from the official file that Ms. Johnson presented us with. Our letter of enquiry and the reply received from Corrections Canada are set out below:

November 14, 1994

The Director
Correctional Service Canada
Information Access
340 Laurier Avenue West (Sir Wilfrid Laurier Building)
Ottawa, ON K1A 0P9

Dear Sir/Madam,

Re: Douglas M. Johnson a/k/a Kathy Johnson
FPS # 069463A

The above individual is currently on parole in Vancouver. She is also diagnosed as being transsexual.

We have indicated our agreement in principle to publishing her story and have her working on it in conjunction with a professional co-author who is herself of transsexual origin. To make the project effective and of value to researchers, guidance counsellors, medical professionals and others, we have examined and intend to quote critical excerpts from the extensive file she obtained from you under the Freedom of Information Act and note that a number of items are stamped "protected" and at least one psychological assessment contained the warning "Confidential-Not to be Reproduced," words which were evidently appended by the consultant. The word "Confidential" has been obliterated, or at least that was the intention.

We believe you have released this material without any caveat on its use, but we would like to know what you consider to be the legal limitations on the use of this material whenever we quote excerpts. We are not interested in exposing ourselves to any avoidable libel situations, the intention at all times being to pursue any use of the material in a critical, analytical but constructive manner.

We know that an understanding of the complex subject of transsexualism is often difficult to achieve, sometimes for philosophical reasons or because of religious limitations. The main thrust of the book is therefore to develop a better understanding of the subject.

In replying we request a copy of the latest policy directive for dealing with transsexuals in the federal prison system.

> *Yours truly,*

> *CORDILLERA BOOKS**
> *S.C. Heal*
> *Publisher*

By letter of November 25, 1994, we received the following reply from the Correctional Service Canada:

Thank you for your captionally noted letter dated November 14, 1994.

I believe your questions focus essentially on one item, namely the confidential nature of the personal records under the control of the Correctional Service of Canada (CSC) that were disclosed to the above named, Douglas M. Johnson a/k/a Kathy Johnson.

In a nutshell, an individual is entitled, within the limitations of the law, to access the personal information that the Government of Canada holds on him.

The personal records that the CSC disclosed to Ms. Johnson constitute the personal information that was disclosable to her. Consequently, the copy of her personal records that was given to Ms. Johnson belongs to her personally. Ms. Johnson is free to dispose of that personal information at will. Therefore, were Ms. Johnson to elect to share, with anyone, the information contained in her copy of her personal records, be it stamped "confidential" or "not to be reproduced," that is her decision to make.

What is said here applies to records disclosed to the subject by the CSC. If the subject accessed personal information from other sources, public or private, please direct your queries to these organizations. Also it is our pleasure to send you, as requested, the attached copy of Commissioner's Directive 800, Section 34 etc. "Sexual Gender Changes."

I hope these comments will be of assistance.

I remain,

Fernand Dumaine
Director, Access to Information and
Privacy Division
Correctional Service of Canada

(*Publishers note: *Cordillera Books* acts collectively for *Cordillera Publishing Company* and *Perceptions Press.* The latter name is an imprint which we use for books in this genre.)

Commissioner's Directive 800, Section 34 etc. governing "Sexual Gender Change" referred to in the Correctional Service was dated 1992-05-11. Subsequent reexamination of Ms. Johnson's file revealed that there is evidently a later version dated 1993-07-15 from which we now quote:

34. The diagnosis of transsexualism shall be made by a recognised psychiatris—expert in the area of gender identity. A referral to such an expert may only be initiated by the institutional psychiatrist following regional approval.
35. Assessment results shall be sent to the Director General, Health Care Services for approval to commence or continue treatment.
36. If an offender has been on hormones prescribed through a recognized gender program clinic prior to incarceration, he may be continued under the following conditions:
a. that the offender be referred to and reassessed by a recognized gender assessment clinic; and
b. that continuation of hormone therapy is recommended by the gender assessment clinic.

37. Unless sexual reassignment surgery has been completed male inmates shall be held in male institutions.

38. Sexual reconstructive surgery may be considered during the offender's sentence, but must receive prior Regional Deputy Commissioner and Commissioner approval.

39. Subject to operational considerations, the institutional head may permit cross-gender dress.

By way of contrast consider the equivalent rules defined by B.C. Corrections Branch in their Manual of Operations - Adult Institutional Services. These were approved April 25, 1994, by the assistant deputy minister and were current Sept. 11, 1994, when received by us. They read as follows:

Introduction 10.01: *Transsexuals are persons genetically of one gender with a psychological urge to belong to the other gender. These persons are characterized by their feeling of discomfort and inappropriateness about their anatomical gender and by persistent behaviour generally associated with the other gender. There is usually a desire on the part of the individual to alter his or her sex organs in order to function as a member of the other sex.*

After a psychological, psychiatric, physical and social assessment, a transsexual living in the community in a stable environment would normally progress through a treatment program as follows:

1. psychological/psychiatric evaluation to assess the degree of the person's transsexuality;

2. *the person lives as a member of the other gender (e.g. dress, hairstyle, etc.) for a period of time (e.g. a few years);*

3. *hormonal therapy is initiated (causing changes in facial hair and body hair growth, breast structure, etc.);*

4. *surgical removal of sex organs (e.g. castration: removal of testes or ovaries, hysterectomy: removal of uterus, etc.);*

5. *surgical reconstruction of sex organs (e.g. penis, vaginal cavity, etc.); and*

6. *application is made to the courts and Vital Statistics Branch of the Ministry of Health for official sex change on birth certificate.*

New Admissions 10.02: Inmates claiming to be transsexuals, who are admitted to provincial correctional centres without previous medical assessment, may request a medical assessment in order to determine:

1. *the validity of a claim of transsexualism; and*

2. *appropriate placement in a male or female correctional centre.*

Such assessment may also be requested by correctional centre staff.

Readmissions 10.03: On re-admission, where a previous medical assessment had been carried out, a reassessment shall be performed to determine the extent of the inmate's progress in the treatment program outlined in 10.01, steps 1 - 6.

Treatment 10.04*: As the required levels of personal support may not be present in a correctional centre setting, it is not expected that progression in the treatment program will occur while the inmate is in custody. However, the inmate will be maintained at the current level of treatment (e.g. if the inmate was taking hormones in the community, the medication will be continued in custody).*

Refusal to Consent to Medical Assessment 10.05*: If an inmate refuses to consent to a medical assessment, the inmate shall be placed in a male or female correctional centre according to the best judgement of correctional centre and/or medical staff based on the extent of the inmate's apparent progress in the treatment program outlined in 10.01, 1-6 in accordance with the criteria set out in 10.07.*

Procedure for Medical Assessment 10.06*: Upon request for a medical assessment, nurse shall be informed and arrangements shall be made for the inmate to be assessed by a medical doctor and psychologist and/or psychiatrist as soon as possible.*

While awaiting such assessment, the inmate shall be held separate from the general population in the correctional centre to which the inmate was admitted.

Following the assessment, the medical doctor shall inform the correctional centre director of the recommended appropriate placement.

Treatment of those inmates confirmed as transsexuals shall follow established medical practice.

Placement 10.07: *Transsexuals who have not progressed beyond step 3 in the process as set out in 10.01 shall be placed in a correctional centre consistent with their originating gender.*

A comparison of the federal and provincial rules reveals the fundamental incapacity of the Corrections Canada rules to manage the needs of transsexual prisoners in a progressive sensible manner. Far too much relies on the judgement of one or two senior officials who have what amounts to the power of God over the prisoner. They appear to have the right to rule without justification of their responses. It would be possible to form a judgement based solely on how such a person might be influenced by a lesser individual exercising his or her discretion based solely on wrong or false interpretations or the exercise without good cause of simple prejudice. Such an example is documented in the recommendations of R.B. Scovill as set out in Chapter Fourteen. With a report like that before them it seems unlikely that the commissioner or his deputy would override the recommendations of a more junior official. Added to that we have already seen examples of how prison doctors lacking specialist knowledge have overridden the recommendations of specially engaged experts.

The federal rules compare very unfavourably with those of the Corrections Branch of B.C. Frankly, one can present little if any argument against the provincial rules. They are sensible, straightforward and leave little to chance. Even a relatively inexperienced official would have no problem in interpreting them. The main point they show up is just how inadequate and antiquated the federal rules actually are. Had author Johnson been subject to the provincial rules as they currently apply it seems probable that the majority of her problems could have been dealt with in a satisfactory manner.

For anyone to claim that the federal rules are justified on the grounds that federal prisoners are in for longer terms for more serious crimes is in our opinion unjustifiable. Common standards of humanity should apply as between federal and provincial institutions. When one links the above rules to the comments of Professor Michael Jackson in his book *Prisoners of Isolation,* the late Dr. Guy Richmond in his book *Prison Doctor* and the report of the recent enquiry of Madame Justice Louise Arbour of the Ontario Court of Appeal to which we have referred in Appendix III, it is not hard to see where the shortcomings in the system have lain and still lie to this day.

* * * * *

Appendix III

The Concept of the Canadian National Health System and Human Rights Considerations

The Federal Health Act was enacted with the clear idea that a national health system would provide common services to all Canadians. It sets out no exceptions which might be taken to apply to those diagnosed as being transsexual. In the execution of the Federal Health Act it is clear that it is hardly a level playing field. The poll of provincial health ministries taken by the Zenith Foundation mentioned in Chapter Eleven indicated variations in handling transsexual procedures from province to province. All claim to adhere to advisory rules laid down by the Clarke Institute of Toronto, the exception being the province of Quebec which has developed separate guidelines.

The Zenith project brought out the fact that not all health officers are prepared to accept anything other than their own concept of what gender dysphoria is. Within the medical profession the key discipline in diagnosing gender dysphoria is psychiatry, with psychology input, and for long it was believed by many and accepted by the churches, for example, that it was wholly a psychological complaint. While disagreement may still remain within these disciplines, informed professional opinion based on solid in-depth research indicates with something very close to certainty that the origin of gender dysphoria is to be found in the prenatal period of the human life and is therefore biological in origin.

When a condition can be written off as being wholly psychological the inference appears to be clear that in some way the subject brought it on himself. He chose this as a way of life like succumbing to drugs or some other temptation. It is reasoned that there are alternatives, most commonly of a religious nature, although no one can define those alternatives in a manner which in any way gives comfort or security to the transsexual, particularly when at the height of his personal crisis. Equally commonly demonstrated are the fundementals of ignorance and prejudice based on faint knowledge and erroneous beliefs.

Why is health care so important to the gender dysphoric condition? Without it long-term depression and psychological distress can ensue which in turn can give rise to physical conditions including those related to severe stress, anxiety syndromes and heart problems and their consequences. The risk of suicide arising from unattended transsexual disorders is also a very real consideration.

We have touched on costs elsewhere but, to repeat, the approximate cost of surgery today is around $10,000. Previously, roughly 25 per cent of this was recoverable in British Columbia under the province's Medical Services Plan. A recent change in the rules now provides full coverage for the entire cost of the operation and hospital care, provided the applicant for coverage has met certain conditions including the life test and has a fully documented history of clinical care. This cost compares to perhaps two to three weeks of confinement to the psychiatry ward for a person suffering from severe depression.

The Report on Human Rights in British Columbia was prepared and presented, at the behest of the Harcourt government of British Columbia, by Professor Bill Black of the Faculty of Law, University of British Columbia in December 1994. It was clear on issues of ignorance. Some 250 organizations made submissions to the committee which held hearings around the province. A frequently recurring issue was the lack of public education on given issues and in many instances this was at its worst in the organs of government. Certainly so far as transsexual people are concerned this has generally been so.

In a telephone conversation between author Castle and Prof. Black soon after his report was released to the public, he asserted that transsexuals enjoyed the same rights as any other citizen in terms of the Canadian Charter of Rights and Freedoms and the protection of its discrimination and equality sections which would likely be so if transsexualism was merely just another illness and was treated as such. We did, however, have difficulty with Black's statement. The empirical evidence indicates that the needs of transsexuals have a very low, if not non-existent, priority when compared to the manner in which the needs of the ordinary citizen are addressed in terms of human rights and health care.

With this in mind a Vancouver organization, the High Risk Project Society, obtained funding from the Law Foundation of British Columbia in 1995 and invited other organizations with associated interests in the transgendered community to join with it in the development of what became known as the *Transgender[11] Law Reform Project.* Represented on the committee were the Zenith Foundation, the Cornbury Society and the Gender Clinic at Vancouver Hospital as well as expert legal counsel.

---

[11] The word "transgender" is now used by some sources in an umbrella sense to cover gender identity disorders other than transsexualism. As our concerns strictly relate to transsexualism we will not make further reference to "transgender," "transgendered," or "transgenderist" in order to minimize confusion.

What has resulted is a study entitled *Finding Our Place*[12] which is believed to be the first intensive gathering of evidence yet undertaken in Canada and certainly in British Columbia to address the twin problems of health and human rights issues right at the grass roots as they apply to the transsexual community. What the study brings out is a variety of issues which clearly indicate the third-class citizenship status of transsexual people. It is not the purpose of this appendix to seek to duplicate the extensive coverage developed by the editorial committee, but the document will be of great value in assessing the relative position of the transsexual community as a component of modern day society. We recommend it as a basis for further research.

Finding Our Place does not intend to take into account the poor position of transsexuals caught up in the prison system. That was not part of its mandate. It would probably take a whole new project to cover this subject, although it also has to be said that there are organizations in Eastern Canada which purport to cover this area in terms of prisoners' rights. When we enquired we received no response so are unaware of any progress they might be making.

The point we are leading up to is that a prisoner in the system has no rights at all in terms of dealing with his transsexual condition. The evidence that transsexual prisoners within a male institution can spell deep trouble for the administration and can be a disturbing influence within the prison population as well as for themselves has been demonstrated more than abundantly within our narrative. Everything about the position of a transsexual within the system

---

[12] *Finding Our Place: Transgendered Law Reform Project.* (1996) Published by the High Risk Project Society, 449 East Hastings Street, Vancouver, B.C. V6A 1P5

is one of condemnation. Condemnation to a prison term as punishment for a crime committed is one thing, as has been noted before, for which we offer no criticism. That is the system and the wrongdoer should take into account the penalty before committing the crime. But condemnation for actually being transsexual is another issue and it is at this point that the system confounds itself and finds that even the ordinary rights of a citizen incarcerated become undermined. We are not suggesting for example that if a transsexual develops a boil on his neck he will not get the same treatment as a non-transsexual prisoner suffering from the same complaint. It is in the areas of adequate specialist treatment and personal security that the transsexual is exposed to never-ending neglect and danger. It is there that the transsexual needs special consideration, as an alternative to injury, including that which is sometimes self-induced and influenced by the most extreme anxiety and stress, as well as suicide.

Author Johnson spent 30 years in the prison system of which about 13 were spent in segregation more or less voluntarily or at least by committing some minor infraction in order to gain access to segregation as the only place where some personal security could be found. In the process, of course, she lost any credits for good behaviour. She had to be anything but a model prisoner to maintain whatever security she could achieve. We suggest that is a very poor, needlessly dangerous and highly contradictory way by which the prisoner is forced to seek security. If the problem was understood and constructive remedies developed through an enlightened approach, much of the danger to the individual could be avoided, mental health could be maintained and heavy wear and tear on the human condition reduced.

Some part of the problem seems to lie in the Clarke Institute rule to the effect that transsexual surgery cannot be undertaken on a prisoner and compensated under a health program while that prisoner remains in an institution or is on parole. We suggest that this is a matter of unusual selection. What other recognizable disease, illness or exceptional condition, such as alcohol and drug addiction, would have been treated in like manner? To the extent that a certain degree of treatment is afforded as laid down in the federal and provincial rules set out in Appendix II, it suggests transsexualism is viewed in a class all by itself, a sort of half and half combination—not enough for full treatment, but just enough to support the idea that it can be kept in a holding pattern. This unsatisfactory state of affairs continues after release from imprisonment and parole takes over. In prison and throughout parole the prisoner is the ward of the system which takes responsibility for his welfare including needed medical services. At the end of the parole period a Provincial Medical Plan takes over, but it remains circumscribed by the special Clarke rule described above. It is a most unsatisfactory way to leave any human condition and because of this it cries out for many improvements in official attitude and treatment.

In that the Clarke rules are, as stated, adopted by all but one province, then that rule becomes a feature of provincial health policy even if out of tune with the equality features of the Federal Health Act or the equality provisions of the Canadian Charter of Rights and Freedoms. The Act does not single out the subject of prison inmates any more than it deals with other particular segments of the Canadian population.

We do not know the actual origin or motivation for the Clarke rule, although it is reasonable to assume that it was instigated at the behest of Corrections Canada when seeking help in developing a policy. Enquiry about the Clarke rule brought no response which might have given some guidance. Very much as an afterthought, literally at the point when this book was going to press, we found *Clinical Management* (detailed in the footnote below).[13] This book, by academics for medical professionals at a similar level to themselves, would not normally be accessible to the broad general public. It is made up of a series of contributions from psychiatrists associated with the Clarke Institute, including Chapter 10 by Robert Dickey, M.D., F.R.C.P. (C). Entitled "Gender Dysphoria and Anti-Social Behavior" Dr. Dickey deals with Criminality in Gender Dysphoric patients. He examines its etiology and moves on to prostitution, but it is when he reaches the subject of Incarcerate Management that he offers some recommendations which frankly surprised us. Unfortunately I cannot quote the entire section in the absence of specific permission from the copyright holder, but the highlights must be noted.

Dickey recommends "freezing" gender dysphorics at whatever level of treatment they are at when entering the prison system. This would mean that a prisoner engaged in a two stage surgical process, i.e. orchidectomy as the first stage to be followed by the second stage vaginoplasty, would be "frozen" as a castrated male if only the first stage had been done. Kathy Johnson, it will be remembered, self-castrated, which in the event did not advance her cause at all, although it was actually the first stage in a gender reassignment surgery. Dickey goes on to recommend that a castrated male should anutomatically be referred to an endocrinologist for hormonal replacement therapy which, without him specifying it, is taken to mean testosterone, which was offered to Kathy after her self-castration. Naturally she roundly condemened this as it was her source of testosterone which she had wished to eliminate.

---

[13] *Clinical Management of Gender Identity Disorders in Children and Adults (1990)* - Edited by Blanchard & Steiner, published by American Psychiatric Press, Inc., Washington, D.C.

Dickey goes on to note "that male patients exaggeration of their feminine characteristics may well have a positive social as well as survival value." By this he is referring to survival in a male institution, which as we have seen has to be one of the most dehumanizing experiences known within our prison system. The cold, cynical logic of the set of policy recommendations laid out by Dickey presumably has the endorsement of the Clarke Institute. It is as cruel as anything that has emerged in this whole account of one human's struggle for survival. Reading through this group of Clarke recommendations is like perusing much of the history of Kathy Johnson's entire prison life. It offers nothing but endless frustration, anxiety and fearfulness for the hapless transsexual prisoner at the same time as it perpetuates a clumsy, uneconomical, and inhuman prison management structure. From the prisoner's point of view the future while in prison can only be anticipated to bring dislocating mental and physical injury as a memento of the prison years.

Regardless of who originated the prison code—the system or its psychiatric advisors—it was evidently adopted as a policy directive which will clearly remain in existence until some new directive overtakes it or Human Rights legislation intervenes.

If the Federal Health Act makes no exception which singles out transsexual people for exceptional treatment, why then does a Clarke Institute rule determine policy in such a narrow sector? Are there any other public policy matters which are dictated by an individual non-governmental agency? Yes, there are. For example a fair number of professions, vocations and business undertakings are governed by specific legislative acts many of which, if not all, have been enacted in response to a clear public need or have been sought by the professions themselves. However, there is a difference. These are usually self-regulatory and in many instances have been requested by the body concerned as a means of governing their own profession and in turn provide protection to the public, in the public interest. Typical are acts governing the real estate industry, the medical, nursing and legal professions, notaries, travel and insurance agents to name a short selection.

If there are other examples of a private medical institution devising rules which govern the lives of other people through their adoption by government agencies as policy rather than through legislation we cannot immediately identify them. The Clarke rule in practice is restrictive, unnatural and has the effect of extending the sentence of the transsexual prisoner, either through the perpetration of acts of defiance as in author Johnson's case, or through discrimination of which there is more than abundant evidence in her story. It clearly confirms the discriminatory practices surrounding the treatment of transsexualism in prison, by comparison with, and by which, no other health matter we can identify is deferred in this manner. We submit that this is a clear transgression of human rights.

Quite fortuitously so far as this book is concerned, just as this appendix was being completed, the report was handed down which resulted from the enquiry headed by Justice Louise Arbour of the Ontario Court of Appeal. This followed the 1994 riot of women prisoners at the Kingston Prison for Women. It lends a great deal of additional credibility to the thrust of this book. We acknowledge that the enquiry had to do with conditions for women in prison, not transsexuals in a male institution, but it did make some sweeping statements which embraced the entire prison structure. Quoting from an article in *Maclean's* magazine of April 15, 1996, written by Sharon Doyle Driedger, Arbour stated:

"The absence of the Rule of Law is most noticeable
at the management level, both within the prison and at

the regional and national levels." Nor did she (Arbour) limit her criticism to the Prison for Women: she said the shortcomings were "systemic" and "part of a prison culture in Canada." Even more damning, she does not trust the correctional service to remedy its own problems. In her scathing report, Arbour concluded that "there is nothing to suggest that the service is either willing or able to reform without judicial guidance and control."

In the same article the writer quotes the Office of the Correctional Investigator, an independent agency that acts as ombudsman for prisoners in federal institutions, which applauded the judge's conclusions.

"Arbour's report is consistent with our findings," said Ed McIsaac, executive director of the office. The article noted that for several years, long before the incident at the Prison for Women, the Correctional Investigator had expressed concerns about the treatment of prisoners—particularly the use of excessive force, segregation and failure to investigate grievances—in reports to Parliament. Is this another example of the infernal Canadian practice of tabling reports which seem to sit where they fall forever and result in no action?

Justice Arbour's quoted remarks apply to all prisoners, not just the women. They speak volumes by way of confirmation of everything that Kathy Johnson has related in connection with her own experience of the system. We now leave it to the reader to judge.

* * * * *

Bibliography

Andersen, Earl. *Hard Place to do Time: The Story of Oakalla Prison, 1912-1991.* New Westminster, B.C.: Hillpointe Publishing, 1993.

Black, Bill (Special Advisor, B.C. Human Rights Review; Minister responsible for Multiculturalism and Human Rights, B.C. Provincial Government). *Report on Human Rights in British Columbia.* Victoria, B.C.: 1994.

Bolin, Ann. *In Search of Eve: Transsexual Rites of Passage.* South Hadley, Mass.: Bergin & Garvey Publishers Inc., 1988.

Blanchard, Ray, Ph.D. and Steiner, Betty W., M.B., F.R.C.P. (editors). *Clinical Management of Gender Identity Disorders in Children and Adults.* Washington, D.C.: American Psychiatric Press, Inc., 1990.

Castle, Stephanie. *Feelings: A Transsexual's Explanation of a Baffling Condition.* Vancouver, B.C.: Perceptions Press, 1993.

Finlay, H.A. and Walters, W.A.W. *Sex Change: Medical & Legal Aspects of Sex Reassignment.* Tasmania: Finlay, 1988.

High Risk Project Society (with backing of the Law Foundation of B.C.). *Finding Our Place: Transgendered Law Reform Project.* Vancouver: 1996.

Hodgkinson, Liz. *Bodyshock: The Truth about Changing Sex.* London: Columbus Books, 1987.

Jackson, Michael. *Prisoners of Isolation: Solitary Confinement in Canada.* Toronto: University of Toronto Press, 1983.

Jay, Monica. *Geraldine: For the Love of a Transvestite.* London: Caliban Books, 1985.

Moir, Anne and Jessel, David. *Brain Sex: The Real Difference Between Men and Women.* London: Michael Joseph, 1989.

North, Maurice. *The Outer Fringes of Sex: A Study in Sexual Fetishism.* London: The Odyssey Press, 1970.

Ramsey, Gerald, Ph.D. *Transsexuals: Candid Answers to Private Questions.* Freedom, CA: The Crossing Press, 1996.

Richmond, Guy. *Prison Doctor: One Man's Story That Must Be Told Today.* Surrey, B.C.: Nunaga Press, 1975.

Walters, W.A.W. and Ross, Michael V. *Transsexualism & Gender Reassignment.* Melbourne, Australia: Oxford University Press, 1986.

Yates, J. Michael. *Line Screw: My Twelve Riotous Years Working Behind Bars in Some of Canada's Toughest Jails.* Vancouver, B.C.: Douglas & McIntyre, 1992.

Index

Books by *Stephanie Castle* in this genre:

Fiction

The Dual Alliance

A Tale of Two Wives

Non-fiction

Feelings:
A Transsexual's Explanation of a Baffling Condition